*To Barb
from Goldie*

# The Joy of Housekeeping

D1571070

# the Joy
## of housekeeping

ELLA MAY MILLER

CHOICE
BOOKS

HARRISONBURG, VIRGINIA 22801

Scripture quotations in this book are from the King James Version of the Bible.

"Money Will Buy" is published by Gospel Publishing House, Springfield, Missouri. Used by permission.

"Happy Task" by Varina C. McWhorter is reprinted by permission from GUIDEPOSTS MAGAZINE, Copyright 1972 by Guideposts Associates, Inc., Carmel, New York 10512.

**A CHOICE BOOK**

Published by Fleming H. Revell Company
in special arrangement with
Mennonite Broadcasts. Choice Books edition published 1975

CHOICE BOOKS are distributed exclusively by Mennonite Broadcasts. The word "Choice" and the portrayal of a man reading a book within a circle are registered in the United States Patent Office. Mennonite Broadcasts, Inc., Harrisonburg, VA 22801.

*Library of Congress Cataloging in Publication Data*

Miller, Ella May.
    The joy of housekeeping.

    Includes index.
    1.  Home economics.   I.   Title.
TX145.M48      640      74-28373
ISBN 0-8007-0714-1

# Contents

# Introduction

Housekeeping is pretty much what you make it—a burden, something you hate. Or . . . .

It can be a source of satisfaction—a challenge, and bring joy to the homemaker.

What makes the difference? The answer is simple—yet profound and difficult: It's basically the homemaker's attitude.

After having said that, there are also other factors —knowing how—accepting it as an essential part of homemaking—and having Someone to help. That Someone is Jesus Christ. He is interested in your everyday routine. You can do everything "in word and deed" to His honor and glory.

These chapters will help you form right attitudes, help you learn how, and direct you to help beyond yourself—thus making housekeeping a joy.

Peace and Joy . . . .

ELLA MAY MILLER

# 1

# Accept Your Role

You suddenly are very much aware of a role change.

Yesterday you were planning your own day. Making your decisions. Scheduling the day according to your job. Spending your own money—for what *you* wanted. Eating on the run. Getting to bed at irregular times. Traipsing over to Sally's house, on impulse.

You've worked through personhood. Accepted yourself as a female. With a unique female biology—glands, organs designed so you can one day conceive a child, nurse it, and tenderly care for it.

*Today*—you live with another adult. One of the opposite sex with different life-style—thought patterns—unique physical and biological needs. Someone else to consider—at mealtime, at bedtime, when you spend money, or have an impulse to leave the house.

You've discovered a completely new life-style. No longer one, but two, with the goal of oneness in purpose, goals, and schedules.

Not oneness in personality but oneness in life-style.

You are a wife. Together you and your husband face the daily situations and daily demands. You are learning what needs to be done, what each one's schedule is, abilities, likes, and dislikes are. You plan how to meet each other's emotional, physical, mental, and social needs.

You enjoy making him joyful. In return he meets your needs.

You experience joys and pleasures. Some conflicts. But together you resolve them.

## INCLUDES WORK

Marriage also includes work. You need three meals a day. This requires cooking, cleaning up dishes and counters. Rooms get messed up. Floors get dirty. Appliances do, too. Clothes need laundering. All this involves work (sometimes hard and unexciting).

Cora confessed after seven years of marriage that she tried to ignore her role. She "hated" housekeeping. She was totally unprepared; furthermore she wasn't about to learn. "Fortunately, I had a very kind and patient husband who put up with me and my immaturity. Even after our two children were born I refused to put myself into my housekeeping work.

"Then one day it hit me—housekeeping belongs to home and marriage and family. It's a part of my life, as a wife and mother. From that day on I've enjoyed it. Prior to then I had refused to admit that housework was necessary. Refused to accept it. I am thankful for this new insight. My husband and family are very happy with the 'new' me."

Kay states it very well. "I've been married seventeen months and have a lovely four-month-old daughter. Housework can be a chore. It's not that I dislike it, only I really don't know how well enough to get everything done the way it should be. Believe me, housework requires as much skill as any business position."

## ACCEPTANCE—THE KEY

Marge confesses, "I want to serve my Lord as choir director, Sunday-school teacher, help in child evangelism as well as participate in community activities. But as for housekeeping, it's a source of discouragement for me. I run away from it whenever I can. I thought the Lord would automatically make me a good housekeeper, but the miracle hasn't happened."

Marge—it'll never happen until you accept that role as a part of the Lord's work. Only in acceptance will you overcome your discouragement and have peace about it. Not in running away, nor in busyness, nor in mere resignation. God's will is perfect, right and good. He included housework in homemaking.

It's demanding, but exciting—depending on your attitude and approach to your role.

A housewife can get bored, become disgusted when faced with the daily tasks. And the next day they begin again.

Marriage counselors have discovered that poor housekeeping is a major factor in many marriage disturbances today.

Housework *doesn't* come naturally.

## A PROFESSION

Keeping house isn't easy. It's difficult and very often complicated. It contains many facets, requires greater expertise than any other career.

Homemaking is a *profession*. It takes skill. Know-how. The ability to organize. A desire to want to achieve.

You need to approach running a house in the same way as a job. You must be serious about your work—and have proper training, or experience.

Have you heard about the young bride who called her husband at the office at 11:00 o'clock? "Honey," she sobbed, "What shall I do? I've boiled those eggs all morning and they still aren't soft!"

A homemaker is boss, manager, employee, in charge of public relations as well as cook, cleaning maid, laundress, and handyman. Besides—she's supposed to be wife—who is companion, friend, lovemate and helper. Later she becomes a mother with all the added responsibilities and privileges of child care.

It's a challenging job. Your preparation as college or university graduate, as an English major, or secretary, or TV producer is no comparison.

It's important for the average homemaker to learn to master the techniques of keeping house. Then she can get the tasks done, and still have time for other activities. (There's one caution—don't allow these other activities to keep you from doing the home activities!)

Without proper planning and schedules and right attitudes, a homemaker is continually frustrated. Never gets on top. But *most basic* to "getting on top" of the daily housekeeping work is to accept that fact that there is *housework* involved—just as Cora says.

Dr. John A. Schindler, author of *Woman's Guide to Better Living,* says that girls should realize before marriage and be prepared for the truth that they will need to do more work (and more difficult work) after marriage than before. He suggests that a mature attitude helps.

## LIKING TO WORK IS A MATURITY

It's bad enough to have to work, but having to work hard and long *without liking it* is a tragedy! Such an attitude dries up one's humor, one's mind, one's enthusiasm—in short, one's life.

So the best thing to do is to learn to enjoy work! Tell yourself that you like to work because you like the end results—a home that's livable and comfy.

You don't begin to mature. You have to learn to turn an adult situation into a benefit rather than into trouble.

When your wash doesn't dry, your sink's full of dirty dishes, a child's in bed with measles, and the baby's soiled from head to foot, you'll just have to tell yourself over and over again, *"I am important."* Then meditate on the joys and satisfaction which a husband, a home, and a family bring to you. There's more involved than just work!

Someone has said, "A mature woman accepts the limits of her choice." You chose to be a wife, perhaps now a mother. Such choices limit you to some restrictions, to some demands that you would not have otherwise. They also include a lot of rewards, privileges and experiences you would not have with other choices.

## REWARDS OF HOUSEWORK WELL DONE

There's no one in the wide world with a more important job than you have in your home! You inwardly thrill as someone comments on your home, family, or husband's ability.

You do receive pleasure from seeing the shiny floor after you finish waxing it—from a tempting meal after you've prepared it—from the neatly dressed children ready for school or Sunday school—from the family project—all completed. From the fun times, work, and worship times together. The list could go on and on, for nearly all your work results in visible, tangible improvement and rewards.

## How To Enjoy Housework

Right attitudes are the secret of happiness while doing housework. Remember, as a housewife you are being useful. Imagine, if you can, if you were never of any use to anyone! Being useful does bring happiness. A grumbling, defeatist attitude spoils your day. You'll be able to do more work without tiring, if you make up your mind to like it. Without even working, *just disliking it,* causes tiredness.

And that's all it takes—just a will to be pleasant and cheerful in the midst of your tasks. No one else can do this for you. It's your choice.

Another attitude that helps you to enjoy your work is this thought: "I can work." Pull it out from time to time. Be grateful for physical strength, for a healthy body.

And finally, start enjoying "work for work's sake." That implies a sense of crusade, or mission—perhaps even a pioneer. It's your God-given assignment! With this idea of liking to work comes a feeling of satisfaction, knowing you have something to do. If you've had to be inactive for a period of time, you know just what I mean.

It's wonderful merely to have something to do. And it does some good. It's worthwhile. There are millions of women living without purpose, without meaning. So keep on telling yourself, "I'm fortunate. I'm pleased that I can work, even do housework!"

Remember you *are* important. A positive attitude will help you accept your role. With this *initial* basic step you can accept and resolve the daily problems and difficulties.

## Love and Creativity

"Studies have shown that homemakers who feel that housework is drudgery and a thankless job will find the work exhausting. On the other hand, women who view homemaking as a labor of love for the family gain satisfaction and a feeling of creativity from providing for the family's needs.

"We hamper our work capacities by frustrations, irritations and impatience, all of which consume three to four times the energy that actually doing the work would take. Inability to make decisions or to take action also consumes added time and energy that could well be spent in getting the job done. Instead of needlessly burning energy through frustrations, find the situations that can be remedied and learn to accept what cannot be changed.

"Worry can poison all forms of energy if it is uncontrolled. Learning to control this energy will lead to a happier way of life. Like everyone else, you have limited energy and great demands on it. So it is important to know what is best for your family and yourself. Spend your energy to achieve these goals with as much caution as you spend the family budget."

> Mattie Kessler
> "From the Woman's Angle,"
> *Cooperative Farmer*

You'll enjoy your role more when you become involved in creative work. There's lots of creative work in housekeeping, but as Clare comments, "Housework can be a drag without the proper spirit and attitude. I find that hobbies and creative things help give me a sense of well-being."

## ENJOY HOUSEWORK

Bertha has accepted her role. The results?

"I have been a homemaker for twenty-five years this month and have five children ages twenty-four, twenty-two, thirteen, eleven and seven. We all enjoy a clean home and I do my very best to keep it that way. The exercise is especially good to keep a homemaker nice and trim. I weigh a few pounds less than the day I was married twenty-five years ago, and attribute it to a good husband who cares enough to compliment me on a clean home as well as a neat and clean appearance around the house. Housework can be very much enjoyed if the homemaker simply realizes how she is needed and how gratifying housekeeping can be with a good healthy approach and a singing love of God in your heart.''

# 2

# A Daily Schedule Helps

"I'm not lazy. But I don't know anything about management. My housework never gets done. There's piles of laundry to be done. The floors are filthy. It's time to get dinner. Can you help me?" questions twenty-year-old Rosie.

Sue complains, "Is there no way to enjoy housekeeping? I never get done with the work until I have to do it all over again. My mom never let me do anything at home. I was always in her way."

## HOME MEANS RESPONSIBILITY

Marriage, home, family—the dream of every normal girl. Her dream comes true. She's up against difficulties she never dreamed of! Thank goodness, this is true. I'm glad I was not aware of *all* that home management and daily routine requires. I've discovered, however, that gradually as I move into the various responsibilities, there is always a way out.

In my parental home there were eight of us girls. I had always worked with others. We took turns washing dishes, cooking, baking, mopping floors, cleaning, making beds.

Later when I worked as maid in other homes the routine

chores were my only responsibility. I enjoyed keeping house. It was a deep pleasure to prepare the meals. I felt a sense of accomplishment in cleaning the kitchen, dining room, living room, bedrooms, and bath. I satisfied creative desires in preparing new dishes. By Saturday noon, all the house was cleaned. The bread, pies, and cake were baked and we leisurely prepared for Sunday.

## LEARNING PROCESS

However, I soon discovered after marriage that *I* was totally responsible for all the chores that had been shared among us girls. Now I was a wife, a missionary wife, and after two years a mother with a multitude of responsibilities and demands besides *housekeeper*.

I tried to do all the baking plus the cleaning on Saturday (as was my earlier pattern) so everything would be spic-and-span for the weekend. Believe you me, I soon discovered that was impossible. I couldn't do everything in one day. It was much easier to schedule certain chores for specific days.

Every homemaker has to go through a process of learning what, when, and how in her homemaking tasks —remembering that hers is a unique situation. No two homes nor two persons are alike. She must learn the basic requirements, needs, and problems she faces in order to make the day a good one—for herself, for her husband, and for each family member.

## JOB ANALYSIS

The first step to better housekeeping is to make a job analysis. For most of us planning is nine-tenths of the job.

What does housekeeping involve?

You deal with both people and things. The people are you and your husband as you begin homemaking. Children enter the picture later. That calls for a change of schedule. Caring for them involves companionship, a social life, child care, education, fun times, rest and sleep, community, school, and church activities.

The things included in homemaking are: care and cleaning of house, upkeep, laundry, selecting clothes and care of them, meals, nutrition, marketing, finances.

You need skillful management and understanding. To harmonize all the many-sided aspects of homemaking is no easy job! Variations must always be recognized. They are always there—daily, weekly, seasonal.

However, there are guidelines (or directives) that will help us housewives get on top of the daily chores—most of the time.

## PLAN A SCHEDULE

Proper housekeeping requires discipline on your part. Written schedules aid you in this. When housekeeping becomes automatic this may be dropped. But that's no license for becoming apathetic. Not at all! You continue to find new and better ways. This helps keep you young.

"What are your recommendations?" you ask. No exact ones can be made since every home and family situation is different.

You've completed your job analysis. Now list the daily chores: preparing three meals a day and cleaning up afterwards—making beds—helping husband get off to work—caring for the children—a period for self-renewal. These are routine but necessary for daily comfortable living.

Some special weekly tasks include the laundry, ironing, baking, sewing, shopping, basic cleaning. These break each day. In addition to these you have seasonal chores. Clothes must be bought or stored. Holiday activities must be planned for. You'll want to spread out the weekly and seasonal jobs so they don't need to be done at one time.

Some overall rules which make for a well-run home are: shopping once a week, with food properly placed on shelves and in refrigerator. Getting at the job at hand and getting it done. In the morning jotting down the day's activities including the special ones. Finding easier ways to get at the work.

If you have children enlist their help. Remember, the small child *wants* to help. Please allow him/her to. At that stage it doesn't make the job easier, but it's helping the child learn about homemaking. A splendid way to develop warm, close relationships.

## A Guideline

Planning a work schedule is a must. At the same time remember, it serves as a guideline, as a basis for your work, and not something which can't be varied. "Schedules appear to be made up of exceptions," says Mary Davies Gillies in *How to Keep House*. She is so right! There is no exact schedule for every home. You must find the one for your situation.

Yes, plan your work. Plan your dinner at the hour best suited to the needs of your husband and children. But don't go to pieces when he can't possibly make it on the minute. There's always something you can find to do. Clean your counters. Start washing the dirty cooking utensils. Keep a devotional book handy to pick up while you wait, or entertain the children. Read to them. Play games or practice music.

You can't run a house on an exact schedule as at the office or school. Evie tries desperately to do this but literally "climbs the wall" every day. Persons just don't fall into your perfect pattern. They are individuals, too.

On the other hand, not to have any schedule ends in confusion. I know a homemaker who laughs at schedules. When the family can't find clean clothes, she quickly buys new cheap garments. If there's no money she does a huge laundry—then complains how tired she is!

## GET AT THE JOB

One secret of managing the home is a knowledge of what's to be done and how to do it. Another secret equally important is getting at the job and doing it.

One young homemaker with three little children was lamenting the fact that she just didn't get her work done. Finally her brother-in-law remarked, "Well, if you'd get at it instead of talking about it so much you'd be done long ago." She resented the statement at first, but after thinking it over she concluded he was right. She wasted too much time talking about the job and pitying herself.

Your attitude is half the work! Allie admits, "The routine of it all used to get me down. I hated to get at my work, I'd procrastinate and piddle around at little stuff. Often the family came home before I had washed the breakfast dishes. My husband was furious. Now I've discovered I can do my work for the Lord. I'm really excited, and have developed a positive attitude. I get at it in the morning and now I have time for hobbies, for my quiet time, and even visiting friends occasionally." Allie has learned a valuable lesson. "Get at the job and get it done." This calls for sorting priorities, and putting "first things first."

You'll also want to have a practical calendar conveniently located. On it jot down any appointment or activity (doctor and dentist appointments, church, school and community activities). You'll need to arrange your tasks around the special activity for the day. Then check the calendar daily.

(I've forgotten to check and once missed an important dinner date.)

## JANE

I've outlined the basic steps to getting at your housework. How does it actually work out in a homemaker's life? Let's peek into Jane's life.

When Jane married she was totally unprepared for housework. She could wash her own lingerie, press a blouse, help prepare a simple dish. That was little help when it came to the family laundry, cleaning floors, or preparing nourishing meals.

She learned a lot in the first year but still felt inadequate. She knew only through experience could she gain confidence and efficiency. From experience one develops a kind of sixth sense which reminds you to disconnect the iron when the phone rings—to lower the heat under the potatoes when the child cries.

Jane wanted her daughter to be better prepared than she herself had been. She felt angry at society which expects its daughters to enter marriage without learning housekeeping skills.

## FACES REALITY

Jane did a job analysis. She listed all her chores—inside the home and outside. She noted the problems of meeting the demands of the children, assisting her husband, meeting her outside activities, and finding relaxed times together with the family.

Next, together with her husband, she worked out a schedule. She experimented for several months until a workable plan emerged. She discovered she could cut out some unnecessary jobs.

Jane also was aware that her answer was not in getting

more appliances. Studies indicate that hours spent in regular housework go up with appliances. The amount of physical energy lessens, but there's more cleaning and more maintenance involved.

It isn't easy to cut out housework, to know what is most important. But making a definite plan for the week helped Jane. She preferred this to trying to do as much as possible in one day in a haphazard fashion.

Remember, "A job well planned is a job half-done."

## New Rewards

Jane found having a schedule reassuring. It helped remove the feeling that floors needed scrubbing the minute they were dirty. She learned to finish a job before going on to the next one. Going about her housework in an orderly fashion gave her more time for herself, for the children.

She now had bonus time each morning—a twenty or thirty-minute period for her own personal needs, or a quiet time with God. This allowed for flexibility, for the unexpected. She had regular play periods with the children. They were happier and not so demanding as formerly. She included them in her chores as much as possible.

Jane's greatest discovery was that a plan removed worry, hurry, and tension from her working hours. It also improved her disposition. Jane says her disagreeable disposition used to drive her daughter away from helping her set the table or dust the furniture. Now they have lots of good times working together.

## Mary's Schedule

Mary's family and situations are different than Jane's. So she has planned her work to suit their needs. Let's peek at her daily schedule:

| | |
|---|---|
| 6:30–8:00 | Breakfast; two children off to school; husband to work. |
| 8:00–11:00 | Baby bathed and fed; beds made; dishes washed; floors swept; laundry started. |
| 11:00–12:00 | A fifteen-minute devotional break; prepare lunch. |
| 12:00–1:00 | Lunch for both her and the baby; playtime. |
| 1:00–3:00 | One-half hour relaxation; jobs her household demands (washing windows, airing bedding and clothes, or putting them away). |
| 3:00–4:00 | Time with children; listening to the day's reports. |
| 4:00–6:00 | Preparing and serving dinner. |
| 7:00–8:00 | Clean up kitchen, children help. |

Mary places in her weekly schedule the social activities: PTA, Homemaker's Fellowship, Prayer Circle, doctor and dentist appointments. At this stage of family life she refuses responsibility or participation in any other continuing activity.

Once a month or more Mary and her husband have an evening out together.

As with Jane, Mary's schedule is only a guide. It's flexible and stretches to include the daily unexpected experiences—visitors, fretful baby, husband's plans, a picnic. She also assigns daily and weekly responsibilities to the children—according to age and ability.

No two schedules are alike, because no two families are alike. Every homemaker needs to plan her work to suit herself and the family. It requires effort, self-discipline and a "want to."

Marge thought when she turned herself over to Jesus Christ that He automatically would help her become a good homemaker. She felt very discouraged about her housekeeping. But no miracle happened. She also says, "I know that all my involvements in Bible study, choir, children's club will be in vain if my house is in constant disorder. I just can't budget my time. I need help."

## I WAS THERE

There was a period in my early motherhood when I felt it was impossible to rise above the daily demands of my family and house. But I had faith in God. I believed He could help me enjoy my housekeeping. This desperate woman cried to the Lord. He heard my cry and saved me from depression, resentment, and hostility. He showed me that homemaking was not a trap. It was a part of His design for family.

To be able to live, every man, woman, and child needs food, protection, clothes; needs a place to be, to sleep; needs each other. Each of us needs a home—an emotional filling station from which to go out and meet the demands and hurts of a cold world—and come back to happiness, joy, peace, security, love.

God taught me home was the most important social unit in society. As goes the home, so goes the community—the church—the nation.

He also taught me that I could do everything—wipe up messes, change diapers, mop floors, help my husband, meet each child's needs—"as unto Him." Whatever I did —whether it was eat, drink, work, play—I could do it to the "honor and glory of God." The motive, the attitudes, the feelings, makes homemaking—*not* the specific chore. *How*, not what or which.

With this revelation and with His Presence alongside of

me I could face my daily responsibilities and do them with a joy, peace, love, and satisfaction.

Housework *is* important. Without it you could not have "family." Learn what's required. Plan for it. Bring God into your planning—into your daily schedule.

*You can enjoy housework. Try it!*

# 3

# How to Clean Rooms

How do you feel about keeping your house clean? Is it a challenge? A job you like to tackle? Or do you procrastinate—snuggle up on an easy chair and watch TV? (Until it's time to get supper? Or bathe the kids?)

Pam laments: "I never get much done, and when I do, the next day my house looks terrible again. I have a messy house but I don't seem to know how to go about cleaning it properly."

You're so right, Pam. A clean house just doesn't stay that way! Dorothy agrees, "I clean today, again tomorrow, and then clean all over again!"

Cleanliness may not be next to godliness, as we've heard in the past, but cleanliness is important to most of us.

## PLEASANT ATMOSPHERE

Cleanliness contributes to the home atmosphere. A dirty, foul-smelling house is no incentive for a husband and teen-ager to come home to.

Jean is desperate: "I never learned the fine arts of housekeeping. I don't know how to clean house and put three decent meals on the table. My mother never bothered teach-

ing me. She could do things faster herself. I often help my
husband who's self-employed. My two little boys make
many demands on my time. Right now I have a pile of clothes
waiting to be washed. The house needs a thorough cleaning
*badly!* This is embarrassing. I'm a Christian but not much of
a witness when people see my dirty house. I need *help.*"

Some homemakers proscrastinate. Some, like Jean, don't
know how to clean. Dot feels it's not worth it. She forgets her
goal—to have an interesting, inviting place for her family.
Incentive is important.

## Too Much

I'm proposing another reason why we housewives often
proscrastinate in cleaning. We have so much to clean. The
more complicated our living gets, the more work is necessary to keep our house clean.

Might some of our housekeeping frustrations lie in the
multitude of gadgets we need to keep clean? If we had less,
would we be happier? Have more time to develop closer and
happier relationships with family, friends, and neighbors?
With those who need us?

During our years as a missionary family in Argentina I was
impressed at the cleanliness of many homemakers, especially of those who lived in mud huts.

Their one wooden table and a few chairs were scrubbed
daily. When the white-washed walls became quite dirty,
they were regularly redone. The dirt floor was daily sprinkled with water, and swept. There was an air of freshness
and cleanliness in the house.

I often thought that to be surrounded by dirt would cer-
tainly be no motivation for cleanliness. But those women
didn't resort to self-pity. To the contrary, many felt sorry for

the homemakers who had so much furniture and furnishings which necessitated so much work!

Scrubbing and cleaning soon completed, they had lots of time daily to be with their children. To sit with mother, sisters, grandmother, and friends chatting and visiting together. Usually knitting garments for the family.

## KEEP GOALS IN MIND

There are various methods to clean your house, but more important are your attitudes. You need an attitude of contentment with what you have, and appreciation for your family. Then follows a sense of accomplishment when you view a clean house—a result of *your* personal efforts.

There are three steps to keeping your house clean and in order. According to Mary Davis Gillies in *How to Keep House,* you need "respect for the job to be done . . . to assemble the right tools . . . and . . . get to work."

I agree; how about you?

Cleaning should never be a homemaker's goal. Her real goal for an orderly home is family pleasure, convenience, and personal satisfaction.

Sally confessed, "I was always upset and irritated and constantly yelling at the family. The house was always in a mess—coats or newspapers draped over chairs, books on the table, on the sewing machine or wherever there was a flat surface, toys on the floor. I felt everything should be in perfect order. But I have discovered that a house is for living. I want my husband and children to enjoy the day. I now straighten up—with their help—at the end of the day. I've learned not to apologize anymore when my friends come over."

Fortunate Sally—she knows that the living room is for

living. She's teaching the children to put toys, puzzles, books, and wraps in their places when they've finished. The family is much happier and is learning a valuable lesson.

## DAILY CLEANUP

Now let's think together for a few moments about cleaning on a daily basis.

A nightly pickup is a good habit, but the daily cleanup comes in the morning, after breakfast is over. You first set the kitchen in order. Doing it first thing in the morning is best, before the day's interruptions begin—before you decide to call someone—before the baby cries, or the small children become restless.

Clear the table. Wash the dishes. Clean the counters. Wipe off the stove so the spilled food won't get all caked and dried up. Sweep the floor. Dust wood floors and waxed floors with vacuum cleaner, or a dry mop treated with a dry-mop spray which makes it more effective in picking up the dust. (Don't use an oiled mop on linoleum, because oil will soften the surface.)

As you begin this daily brushup, open a window for a few minutes. Let a bit of fresh air float in the windows. This is also a good antidote for stale smells, smoke, and dust. This my father taught me. He always got up first in the morning and aired the house as he fixed the fires. During warm weather, some windows were always open.

Now move into the other rooms. You'll next empty waste paper containers—fold the newspaper and put in its place —vacuum where necessary—arrange top of desks. Then move into the bedrooms.

It's good here, also, to let in some fresh air as you make beds and pick up clothes lying around. Your older children may keep their own rooms in order; this is good. If you are responsible for them—let the smaller children tag along. They'll be delighted to help you. This is true in the many other daily routine chores.

## KEEP UP WITH LITTLE THINGS

For the homemaker who works outside the home, you can't leisurely go about the daily cleanup. You can't let the whole task get you down—can't let it grow too big for you to handle—and then just cop out! So do yourself a favor.

Keep up with the little things before they get the best of you (of course—this is a good idea for each of us!). Face one room at a time. Have some jobs you take care of everytime you're in that room.

Pick up magazines and newspapers after you're through with them. Put them out of the way on the racks or shelf designated for them. Put your dirty clothes in the hamper before you're tempted to let a pile accumulate. If you keep up with the little things as you go through the daily routines of living, the job to approach cleaning the whole house doesn't seem nearly so huge.

You've already eliminated the clutter—now all you have to contend with is the dust and dirt that accumulated since the last cleaning you did. Of course if it's been a month since you last faced the dust—then you might have another mountain to climb. But *if* you can keep on top of things—*if* you try to spend a few minutes straightening regularly—it will be easier for you.

## WEEKLY CLEANING

Your weekly cleaning will include thoroughly vacuuming floors, wiping soiled spots, dusting, cleaning window sills, thoroughly cleaning the kitchen appliances, maybe a quick mopping of vinyl or linoleum floors. You may need to rotate cleaning the appliances—one week the refrigerator, the next week the stove, and so on.

Some weeks cleaning includes washing windows. Have you tried using rubbing alcohol (be sure it does not contain glycol) instead of the expensive window cleaning solutions? I saved a squirt bottle and fill it with alcohol. It does a marvelous job, and dries quickly. I also prefer to dry the window with newspaper. Crumple up one-fourth of a page and use it instead of a cloth. It leaves no lint.

Some weeks you'll wax floors.

(By the way, have you ever tried wearing an apron with huge pockets in which to keep your dust rags, brushes, polish? The things you pick up? Some homemakers keep all their cleaning supplies on a small table with wheels and push it as they go from room to room.)

## SPECIAL CLEANING

Besides our daily and weekly cleaning, there's special cleaning time. We seem to accumulate so much "stuff." Dirt and cobwebs accumulate. Closets, walls, and drawers need straightening out. The basement or attic are full and overflowing. It's a long task!

Beulah writes:

"Do you have any hints and helps on housekeeping and home management? My trouble is to know what to keep and what papers and clothes to throw away, and get organized. I am one of those collectors who hates to throw anything away I might want to use or read sometime later.

"Now I know, I must get rid of the excess before I die or the Lord comes, whichever comes first. My children all have plenty to do in taking care of their own homes and families without sorting my things. Any helpful hints you can give will be appreciated.''

We identify with Beulah, don't we? I don't know how you would answer her, but I can share from my experiences.

I do collect or save some items for "future use." So there does come the time for thorough sorting. I lay aside newspapers for the recycling organization. Some magazines we save. The rest are discarded. The clothes no longer wearable I give to the Goodwill Industry. Those that still contain wear I give either to the Salvation Army or to our church relief agency. Occasionally, I give appropriate clothes to individuals, victims of a fire or a personal need I'm aware of.

## Yearly Housecleaning

Do you houseclean once a year? What is your method? "It isn't easy to keep a house decent and in order," says Grace. "But I don't houseclean once a year. Only my sixty-five-year-old grandmother does that! I try to maintain a clean house on a day-by-day basis.''

Grace's idea about cleaning house is typical of the majority of homemakers that I know. She tries to keep her house looking reasonably neat. She's not bothered by a bit of clutter. Her regular routine includes vacuuming, dusting, and wiping off finger prints. When she entertains and has family and friends visit, she more thoroughly cleans—such as windows, walls, throw rugs and curtains. With such a schedule she keeps her house spring-cleaned all year.

Some homemakers focus on one room each month and give it a complete cleaning—cleaning the walls with a soft brush, or sweeper, wash windows, clean shelves, cup-boards, or closets. This eliminates a house all torn up during a seasonal cleaning.

I've discovered I can clean a shelf or drawer as I wait on some family member to come for meals. Depending on what I prepare, if it's a quick meal, I can do some cleaning while preparing a meal. There does come the day when I set aside larger portions of time to clean remaining cupboard shelves, drawers, also closets, and dresser drawers. This calls for sorting out the usable from junk I seem to collect.

## CLEANING METHODS

Let's think about methods of special cleaning.

Use your favorite cleaner on rugs and carpets—the liquid or powder method. You may wish to rent floor machines to help you do the job. Have a stain remover handy to clean stains.

For your wood floor use the new solvent-base cleaning waxes that clean and polish in one operation. To remove black shoe marks, lightly rub with steel wool. There's also a new cleaning-polishing wax floor finish for your linoleum, vinyl, or asphalt floors. If layers of wax have collected, use a wax remover, according to directions.

To clean your wood furniture use a cleaning-type furniture polish and use according to directions.

Use your vacuum cleaner to dust your upholstery. To remove soil on arms or back of chairs and sofas, use spotting agents that dry to a powder. Choose a warm breezy day to clean so you can leave windows open. This speeds the drying process.

To clean walls and ceilings regularly, use the vacuum cleaner. For cleaning painted surfaces, use your favorite cleaning solution, using a sponge mop.

Send the drapes to the cleaner, unless they are ones you can wash.

## CLOSETS

If a limited closet space is a problem for you, consider reorganizing the items you have there now. While you're cleaning and have everything out of the closets or off the shelves, take a good look at the room you *do* have. Is there any way that rearranging these items will make better use of the space? Maybe changing things around will give you more room. Do you have items there that don't need to be there? Put those things that you seldom use in the back or in the areas that are less accessible.

If your husband or one of the older boys is talented at making repairs, he might be able to provide a quick simple solution by adding another shelf.

## FAMILY HELP

There are some jobs that most women just can't handle themselves. Pulling out the stove and refrigerator, moving heavy furniture, flipping large mattresses—these house-cleaning jobs require the help of someone else. A neighbor or relative might be available, but often your husband is the one you need to help get the job done.

Let it be pleasant. Make the job something he doesn't mind helping you with. If you nag him about it, he won't really enjoy helping you. But if you are considerate of his schedule and tender in your request, he'll be much more willing to offer a hand. And let him know you appreciate his help.

And if you're like me, you'll probably get the urge to rearrange the furniture when you houseclean. If you enlist your husband's aid, try not to change your mind too often. It will be much easier on both of you!

Enjoy yourself. Face cleaning as a challenge—not a chore. If you and your husband work together, or you and the children, be sure to thank them for their help. The satisfaction of sitting down in a clean fresh house will be something you'll all feel good about.

## THE REWARDS

The looks and smell of a clean room is reward enough for me. It lifts my spirits and helps me attack the rest of my tasks. I soon forget the work it takes.

Just as the rooms of my house accumulate dust, dirt, and trash and become soiled, so do the rooms of my mind. I quickly accumulate criticism, complaints, quick and harsh judgments, attitudes of rejection, bitterness and unlovely ideas. I need to apply the perfect cleanser—the blood of Jesus Christ—and become clean and pure. He is available. Doesn't cost me a cent—only my will.

We enjoy a clean house, don't we? But let's not make that our goal. Our goal is happy family living.

# 4

# An Attractive Place

Some homes attract you at first glance. Others repel you
—not necessarily because one is new and the other old.

I've seen very attractive old houses. Some new ones are
unattractive. Much depends on one's individual taste, one's
preferences, likes, and dislikes. I recall seeing a millionaire's
mansion—anything but attractive to me. It was costly, but to
me the dark brown exterior, trimmed with a darker brown,
just wasn't attractive.

Making your home attractive doesn't necessarily mean
spending a lot of money. Basically, I define attractive to be
neat, cheerful, pleasant, the yard and surroundings "kept
up."

### An Old Farm House Transformed

For several years on our way to church we'd drive past an
old, unpainted farm house. The porch roof was falling down
on one end. The steps rotted. Junk covered half of it. Half of
the shutters were gone or hanging by only one nail. The yard,
too, was in shambles—weeds and high grass only partially
hid the discarded stove, wheels, several wornout farm im-

plements, boards, and wire. One or two small outbuildings barely survived.

I frequently remarked about the place, for it was conveniently located—on a much-used highway, not too far from the city, "That house has possibilities. I like the architecture. Wish we had money to buy it, and fix it up."

Then, to my joy and surprise, one Sunday we noticed much of the trash was gone from the porch and the yard. Part of the weeds had been mowed. "Someone else is living there," we concluded. Sure enough, each Sunday we would note beautiful changes: the porch and shutters rebuilt; a new paint job, the yard landscaped with bushes, trees, shrubs, flowers. I marvel at and enjoy the transformation which took place within the past ten years. The changes came gradually as the family could find time and money to work at the improvements together.

To make a place attractive requires a goal, lots of effort, and discipline to get it done and to maintain it. The rewards far outweigh what you personally put into it. You sense satisfaction and accomplishment when you personally are involved. It's worth any effort—whether it's inside or outside the house.

## WHAT YOU CAN DO

An attractive place need not require a lot of remodeling and fixing up, or painting. It's simply doing what you can do within your budget and ability to keep things in order, and in place. When the children were at home they helped mow the lawn, trim grass, weed flower beds, dig up bulbs in the fall, replant early spring, and help tend a variety of rose bushes. Now they're gone. I've planted perennial flowers which come up from the same root stock without effort on my part each spring and summer.

In front of the house it looks almost like a jungle (as my husband says). The honeysuckles, ivy, day lilies, a cedar tree (seedling) and other bushes and shrubs have taken over. One is a large asparagus stalk with its fern-type branches in the summer, and red berries come fall. I lack the time to carefully trim, and reseed. On the other hand, I like it. The "natural" look has its own beauty!

## UNEXPECTED PLACES

A place can be attractive in the most unlikely areas. I'm thinking of a slum area in New York City: street after street of coal-dust-black brick buildings with narrow street entrances—flights of grimy stairs lead to rooms on various floor levels, up to five or seven floors. Garbage on steps, and flies, and nonfragrant odors. All very unattractive, but upon opening the door to a home we occasionally visit, I see a completely different picture—shiny floors—clean windows and curtains and kitchen counters—beds made—artificial flowers appropriately placed on shelves and tables—brightly colored pictures hung on the wall. It is an attractive place!

In another area of the city one family cleaned up their small porch and steps. They washed windows, inside and out. They planted window boxes with blooming geraniums and petunias. The transformation was fantastic. It caught on. And before the summer ended, window boxes full of blooming flowers adorned every home in the block. The entire neighborhood took pride in keeping the outside entrance, the porch, and sidewalk clean.

## BEING ORDERLY AND CLEAN

To have an attractive place requires "a place for everything" so when you or the family have finished using the article, there's a place to put it.

It means keeping things orderly. I'm not suggesting children's playthings always stacked neatly in a box, nor every book and magazine in the correct place. The family can each be doing his or her thing—reading, playing games, sewing, doing homework (and all that implies)—and the place can still be attractive. Rather, it's not dropping everything just where he/she used it. It's "riddin' up" at the end of the day (at least every other day), and a weekly cleaning. It's taking care of dirty clothes, dirty floors, and dirty dishes when necessary.

I recall visiting in a very poor mud hut in South America. It was attractive. The thatched roof was new. The ground surrounding the hut swept clean, and hard. The mud floor inside was cleanly swept and sprinkled with water to lay the dust. The wooden table and benches were neatly scrubbed. A small glass set on the table containing lovely cactus flowers. The place was attractive!

## ATTRACTIVE INSIDE

You don't always know what you're getting into when you begin to make the rooms attractive—like several years ago when I decided to paint the living room. It isn't a large room, so I felt capable of doing the job. The appropriate time arrived—when the family, all but one son, were gone for several days. I began the project late afternoon, after completing my daily responsibilities, painting and moving furniture. I worked till late at night. It took much longer than I had anticipated. Besides I was stiff and sore for a week! But all the effort and bodily aches and pain were worth it. Every time I went into the room I was pleased.

You need to consider color schemes, type of furniture, and furnishings in the attractive home. An unplanned room that just happens doesn't look as neat as a well-decorated, planned room.

Basic is a simple color scheme to hold it together. You'll want a good transition of color from one room to the next. The accessories and furniture should be in good taste, and compatible in style.

## CREATIVITY

You may not have a choice in selecting furniture for each room where every piece matches. Don't let this disturb you. The different pieces can be compatible. You may cover a settee or easy chair with an attractive loose cover that hides it as a misfit.

Curtains need not be expensive. In one home I was amazed to see lovely towels at the kitchen and bathroom windows. The family had just moved and there was no money for new curtains and drapes. A pair of lovely flowered bed sheets graced the picture window. They hoped to be able to get the drapes and curtains within several months. In the meantime, the family enjoyed privacy when they desired it.

## REMOVE CLUTTER

Some rooms are very unattractive with too much stuff occupying the once-empty spaces on tables, shelves, and bookcases. They're treasured gifts from favorite friends or relatives. Or souvenirs collected from your travels. Some are pretty. Others are kept because of memories.

Such stuff only clutters a room. Requires dusting and special care whenever you clean. For a well-groomed look, put the small "junk" into a box. You can pull it out occasionally, look it over, and revive the sentiments behind each piece. If possible, provide a display case for souvenirs collected from travels at home or abroad.

Some authorities suggest clearing away all empty vases. Bring them out only when they hold flowers. They also caution not to overdo it with flowers. A center bouquet with one or two small ones is enough in one room.

Did you know that proper storage space helps eliminate clutter? Provide a place for books, magazines, knickknacks, records, collector's items, sewing, and games. Then they're not likely to be lying about all week long.

"What about lamps?" you ask. Lamps should serve a purpose. They are a source of light to enable you to see. At the same time they should add to make the room attractive.

Select pillows and chair cushions to harmonize with the basic color scheme—to provide comfort for the person using them.

## PLANTS AND FLOWERS

Plants add interest and color to your rooms. They can, with proper care, be beautiful in planters as room dividers or in other places not close to windows. Agriculture Department scientists warn that foliage you put in planters may become sick-looking because of insufficient light. Plants can be grown successfully, if you water and fertilize them correctly and provide artificial light when necessary. Contact your local extension service for advice on your particular plants. The requirements vary depending on the variety.

Words of advice written back in 1870 still hold good today: "Love your flowers. By some subtle sense the dear things always detect their friends and for them will live longer and bloom more freely than they ever will for strangers."

Here's Naomi's suggestion:

A little citrus "tree" started from grapefruit or orange seeds makes things look more "outdoorsy" and costs nothing. Or take a chunky piece of driftwood, scrub with a brush and Lysol or Clorox water. Rinse and let dry. Drill a hole deep enough to hold the stems of artificial flowers (choose the most realistic flowers you can find in a color that complements the mood and the room). Practice placing the flowers on the wood in the most interesting and attractive manner before choosing where to drill the hole with your electric drill. Cut stems with wire cutter, insert stems in hole (or holes) and fill with white glue. Arrange the flowers to cover the insertion point, but don't completely cover the wood. Pink or violet flowers look lovely on silvery wood, "wild" red roses on a brown one. I have several and the most expensive one cost me only thirty-nine cents.

Thanks, Naomi. We love you for sharing your beauty secret with us.

## USE THINGS YOU LIKE

Use the things you like—your pretty things, the nice things you're saving. Saving for what? For whom?

Recently in rummaging through a box of "memories," I ran across a lovely set of toy aluminum cookware I received as a Christmas gift when I was ten years old. I never used them. They were too nice. What a lot of fun I missed!

A few years ago I visited a cousin who was using family heirlooms and enjoying them. She had given her mother's wedding china to her married daughter, so she could use them while her daughters were growing up. They'd then appreciate the dishes when they would be passed on to them.

Sarah uses her lovely things daily. She serves milk from a lovely anniversary gift—a pottery milk pitcher. She's glad to discard the milk carton from her table. She has learned the joy of using things she likes.

I'm enjoying some treasures I had stored away for many years—embroidered place mats, a gift from a brother when he returned from Korea—some glass dishes—a quilt made by my grandparents. I only wish I had used them occasionally through the years—to familiarize my children with them, and to convey in more tangible ways the feeling I have for beauty and family ties. If I don't share them with my family, after all, who am I saving those lovely things for?

## THE ATTRACTIVE YOU

I can't conclude this chapter without mentioning the attractive *you*. Your house may be neatly groomed, with adequate storage space, lovely furnishings and appropriate accessories, but a grimy and disorderly housewife can spoil the lovely appearance.

I'm not suggesting you go around all day dressed in party clothes. Not at all! But after you finish the dirty work —scrubbing, sweeping, cleaning, or working outside—dress neatly. Your family will love you for it.

One homemaker, accustomed to appear in a housecoat until noon, was challenged to dress before breakfast. To her surprise, her toddler clung closely to her all morning. He refused to let her out of his sight. The mother was puzzled, until it dawned on her—he was fearful that she was leaving, because her usual pattern had been to dress just before running errands, going shopping, or to the beauty parlor, or to her clubs. The child soon adjusted to her new pattern of living and joined the rest of the family in their increased admiration and respect for their attractive wife and mother.

*Home* is an emotion-packed word. If love and joy and harmony are there, if it's a place the children and parents love to come to, then it's an attractive place. Not only the physical and material appearance, but also the moral and spiritual atmosphere is important. How you live, the kind of husband-wife relationship and parent-child relationship, how you face joys and sorrows, kindness, honesty, fun times, work, and worship—all these help make an attractive home. A home that allows Christ to control and direct also attracts persons to Him.

> Who seems to create
> The atmosphere of the home—
> > Of joy, or gloom . . .
> > Of love, or hostility . . .
> > Of creativity, or sameness . . .
> > Of beauty, or ugliness . . .
> > Of welcome, or rejection—
> Who?
> You, homemaker.
>
> God has given the key
> To unlock the door
> To attractive family living—
> It's Christ in you.
>
> Take it from His hand.
> He will help you make
> Your home attractive and loving—
> Reaching out a welcome
> To family and friends.

# 5

# A Kitchen That Functions

What, to you, is the most important part of your kitchen —the dishwasher—the windows?

A friend of mine reported viewing a TV show where five leading ladies were asked the question I just asked you. Each lady had a different response.

Among the answers were: dishwasher, mixer, padded floor, knives. Each individual's personality showed up. That's okay. It's the way it should be. What you prefer in your home doesn't have to be the same as what your neighbor prefers.

There are basic kitchen needs and conveniences that help each of us do a better job; yet within these basics we can still retain our individualism.

## BE SELECTIVE

Mary Ethel, a home economist, says you should be very selective with what you put in your kitchen. She suggests you select only those items that you use. That's a good idea.

It seems I have accumulated gadgets and items I don't use anymore, or very seldom have used. Recently I've cleaned out several drawers and shelves and discovered by taking out unused items I had room for the usable ones.

Today's housewife is bombarded with scores of new products which are supposed to save time and energy in the kitchen. Personally, I've become rather skeptical of them. I have some which I've used only once. It takes me longer to assemble the gadget, wash it, and put it away than to use my own familiar method!

I'm aware, however, that something I don't use may be just the thing for you. Something you have that is valueless to you, someone else may enjoy using. So—be yourself and select only the items you are comfortable using.

## YOUR KITCHEN

Have you ever been in the kitchen of a friend and wondered how she ever manages to get along efficiently?

You think to yourself, *If I had to work in her kitchen, I'd go crazy! She doesn't have nearly enough cupboards.* Or, *Her stove's too far away from the sink, not even within reach. Yet she manages to get along.*

Some women just don't have a choice. You may not. You and your husband may be recently married. Regardless of age, you may rent or live on a limited budget—situations that do not allow redecorating.

How do you react? Do you dread every minute you have to spend in that hideous kitchen of yours?

Stalking around, yanking furiously on the cupboard door that sticks, ramming your hip into the edge of that cabinet that just isn't in the right place. Muttering to yourself, you get the salt out of the cupboard only to discover that the noodles are boiling over—and in your rush—you burn your fingers.

Is that how it goes?

If things can't be changed, don't fight it. Accept your kitchen as a fact of your life—a place where you need to spend a certain amount of your time each day. Try to make the best of it. Maybe you could rearrange the items in your cupboards to avoid as many trips to those areas of your kitchen that are irritating. Don't dwell on the inadequacies of your kitchen; think about the good you're doing there. You'll save energy and be more relaxed. You might learn to enjoy it.

## WELL-LIGHTED

What do you like about your kitchen? I'm sure each of us housewives has our own personal taste as to what we consider the most important items in our kitchen.

Since I spend so much of my at-home time in the kitchen, I especially appreciate my windows. It's great to see the mountains, the woods, the neighbors' lovely flowers, the people, and cars passing on the street as I go about my work.

However, I do realize many kitchens have windowless walls, but are well-lighted with other types of lighting. Plenty of light makes the jobs easier.

To me this is important: a well-lighted, interesting kitchen. You can create a beautiful atmosphere with lovely pictures, bright-colored ceramic plaques. Also tack pretty cards, Bible verses, or a poem above the sink. As you wash the dishes, prepare the food and clean counters, you can feed your spiritual self with beauty and with God's thoughts. Light-colored walls, brightly colored tea towels and place mats can add a happy touch to the kitchen.

## KITCHEN ARRANGEMENT

How about the arrangement of your kitchen? Are you satisfied with it? Whether there's prospect of remodeling or any change, or not, it's well to understand the basic composition and equipment of the kitchen.

Authorities say that you should never sacrifice efficiency for decorations. Too many women believe if the kitchen is pretty, it's what they need. The kitchen basically is a work space, and should be planned accordingly. Keeping this foremost, the homemaker doesn't need to sacrifice efficiency.

A kitchen needs three work centers—refrigerator-preparation, sink-dishwashing, stove-serving. These are needed to do kitchen chores. If arranged properly, they decrease the work load and allow for greater efficiency.

You probably noted that the sink area is placed in the center of these work spaces—and rightly so. You need the water in your food preparation and again for cleaning the dirty dishes. A double sink is convenient if you do not have a dishwasher. However, many kitchens, (mine included) have only one-well sinks, so I use a divided dishpan.

## Efficiency

The refrigerator and preparation counter beside it is the most used combination of equipment. This work counter should be at least thirty-six inches long. It's best to have the refrigerator door open by the work counter. It'll save carrying foods across the door when you put them in the frig, or take them out to use.

Authorities suggest the range can stand against a wall by itself if something has to be isolated. In that event, you may want to place a small, wheeled table near the stove when you're ready to serve the food.

These three major areas would be placed around the three sides of the room—making the work area in the form of a *U*. This allows for an eating area in the other side.

Eating space is essential in the kitchen area. It may not be an elaborate breakfast nook or lovely breakfast set, but just a counter. Whatever it is, it makes serving meals a lot easier, and brings the family closer together.

Storage space is also essential. If there aren't sufficient built-in cupboards, you can purchase narrow, tall cabinets. They don't take up a lot of space, but do provide a lot of storage room.

## LOCATION

Where is your kitchen located? In an isolated end-of-the-house area?

That's been the traditional place for a kitchen, but designs are changing, and I, for one, am happy about it.

Many kitchens today include play areas for the children, a couch, desk, and sewing facilities. It's the place for family living. While mother prepares the meals, she keeps an eye on the small children. Husband has a place to relax or do his paperwork. Older children can study or play games.

A friend of mine remodeled their house, tore out a wall between the kitchen and adjoining dining room, in order to have this family-style kitchen. They built a fireplace in the center of the room. The family is delighted with the togetherness they have. She reports that they seldom go beyond the kitchen. That's where they usually entertain their friends.

You should choose convenience and comfort ahead of beautiful decorating. However, it's usually possible to combine the two.

## MAJOR APPLIANCES

Do you have all the major appliances you need? If not, let me suggest that you carefully study your needs before you purchase an appliance. Determine which, if any, will best serve you. Then shop around comparing different brands and prices.

*Carefully* read the book of instructions. Keep it in a file drawer, or in your desk, along with other instruction books. Operate the appliance according to instructions, and keep it clean, and it will give you many years of good service.

A home economist recently advised a group of homemakers not to be in a hurry to buy new inventions. Let them be proven first. As an example, she mentioned the microwave oven. After several years it is still in the experimental stage.

You'll need sufficient outlets located conveniently. If your kitchen is like mine (with only half-enough outlets), you can purchase an extension outlet strip to place on your counter. It has room to plug in several appliances, but don't overload the circuit.

If you want things within quick reach and have the wall space, put up a pegboard and hang up many items, like —small pots and pans, strainer, measuring cups, large spoons, spatulas, to mention a few.

## Discontent

Perhaps right now you're staring at your kitchen walls, dreaming of the kitchen you'd like to have. Many housewives do that.

Do you really think that redecorating the kitchen will improve your cooking? Won't the cook be the same—even if the kitchen is new! What is it really that will make you happy?

It's so easy to camouflage our real desires with superficial wants. Maybe what you really want is something much deeper: appreciation of your work from your husband and family—consideration.

Maybe you deeply desire more companionship—more time to share with your family. Maybe you're plain bored and want to redecorate for the sake of change.

Look back a few years. You probably got by on much less than you do now. Maybe life is much better now. Maybe now is the happiest time of your life. But if you look back and wonder where the joy and excitement went, then take a long hard look. Look around you. Your kitchen may be more luxurious than you thought. Maybe conveniences aren't as important as you think.

I'm not saying that your desires for home improvement are wrong. I'd only urge you to ask yourself some serious questions. Is this thing what I desire most, or am I searching for something much deeper—something that may be hard to admit? What is it deep inside that will make me the happiest?

Then ask yourself if you're willing to take on the financial burden for improvements. Will that money spent cut out activities that are important to family relationships? Have I made luxuries a necessity? Do I *need* it as much as I think I do?

## BEAUTIFUL ATMOSPHERE

When we're honest—many of us have a pretty good life, while much of the world lives in poverty. Relationships with people and with God make life enjoyable. *Things* can't do it for you.

I still don't have my dream kitchen. When I find myself beginning to be dissatisfied, I look up—beyond the immediate—and thank God for the many things I enjoy in my kitchen. I remember that family could never exist without a kitchen. It's necessary to daily living. It's probably the most important room in my house.

The kitchen is a very necessary room in your house. Make it comfortable. But most important, create a beautiful atmosphere. Let God's love, joy, and beauty flow through your hands and heart as you perform the kitchen chores.

# 6

# Joy of Creative Cooking

Cooking can be fun, be creative, and bring satisfaction to you.

Or—it can become mere routine. You get in a rut—never varying dinner from the traditional potatoes, meat, beans. Perhaps hot dogs, potato chips, pork and beans.

Granted, that's simpler. Easier to prepare. Doesn't demand too much thought or energy. Get the beans from the shelf. Open the can with the electric can opener. Pour them in a pan and heat them. (Some serve them cold.) Unwrap the wieners and broil or boil them. Place the bag of chips on the table, the loaf of bread still in the wrapper. Add a bottle of ketchup and mustard. Then call, ''Meal's ready!''

You don't have to concentrate much while preparing that kind of a meal. It's repetition. Has become routine. In fact—you don't even have to do that! Just pack up the kids, hurry to a drive-in, and pick up a quick bite.

There's nothing wrong with the foods I've mentioned —nor your approach to eating them. In a pinch—sure—it's great to go out for your meal; it's commendable to be able to prepare a quickie, when necessary.

It just isn't very creative—or challenging.

Creative cooking does something to your status as homemaker. It does this for me to hear my husband or one of the children comment, "Hey, the meal's great. You can try that recipe again!" It gives me a good feeling, a satisfied feeling, a feeling of accomplishment.

## CONSIDER LIKES

A wife will want to learn to prepare the foods her husband enjoys.

The story is told that a starry-eyed bride of a few weeks wanted to prepare a delicious breakfast. She arose early and worked hard. After twenty dirty pans she had prepared a fancy breakfast for two.

Breakfast consisted of apple candy muffins supreme, a fluffy puffy omelet with fruit sauces, a dish called Chipped Beef Enroute (decorated with stars cut out of pimento). She dolled up the grapefruit with maraschino cherries, mint leaves, and marshmallows. Then set the table and called her husband.

He was less enthused than she as he looked at the pretty breakfast. Then in a tone of voice she had never heard before he said, "Darling, I love you. You had a nice idea, but any idiot knows that a man wants bacon and eggs for breakfast, or ham and eggs, or maybe sausage and eggs, but not this tearoom stuff!"

Naturally, the bride left the table in tears. But she was a wise woman. She learned not to waste her time and energy in preparing food her husband didn't enjoy eating.

## A LOST ART?

Scientists predict that by the year 2000 so-called convenience foods will replace today's prepared foods. They will come premeasured in proper sizes and portions. Today's frozen dinners will look as though they belonged to the dark ages.

Snacks and treats children today enjoy will be demanded items on the kitchen shelf. Foods will come prepared to the extent that a mother will ask family members what they want. She'll then press several buttons on the stove computer and relax. They'll no longer eat as a family but as convenient to each one's schedule.

For a husband to treat his wife to dinner, it'll have to be a trip out of the country.

This sounds great to meet the demands of our rapid age, but what about the advantages of the art of cooking? Like unity—sitting around the table together and conversing? or the relationship of mother and daughter (or son) in the floury mess in the kitchen while baking cookies? or the entire family experimenting together?

Cooking can be a creative joy for any homemaker—when she accepts it as a privilege. In preparing wholesome meals and making mealtime a happy time, she cooperates with God in helping her family build healthy, strong bodies.

## MEN SHARE COOKING

In some homes, the husband enjoys cooking more than does the wife.

One man who knew how to cook was asked, "Can you cook?" To the friend's surprise he replied, "Sure, I can cook! But—I go somewhere else to eat!"

This reminds me of a college classmate who worked in the school snack shop. He spent most of his time preparing hamburgers, hot dogs, and toasted cheese sandwiches for the students. One day just before quitting time he approached the manager, "Fix me a hamburger, won't you?"

The manager looked at him in surprise, "What's the matter? You've been fixing them all afternoon."

"I know," he replied, "but I just can't eat one that I make myself!"

Some men do enjoy cooking. Some enjoy eating what they prepare. However, in the home where it's up to the wife to cook the food, she should enjoy it!

Dr. Samuel Johnson wrote, "A man is in general better pleased when he has a good dinner upon his table than when his wife talks Greek."

In my estimation, this truth hasn't changed. To be sure, men help in kitchens, but no man refuses to eat the food his wife prepares with love—because she cares for him, and wants to please him.

## PLANNING MENUS

Some housewives carefully plan the week's menus ahead of time.

Ruth likes this approach. She does her planning on Monday night, before she makes up her grocery list for Tuesday's shopping. She prefers to shop early in the week, to avoid the crowded stores on Friday and Saturday. Some women prefer to shop the weekend when most stores run specials.

In planning her menus, Ruth checks her food supply to see what she has on hand. At the same time she notes the items that are low and adds these to her grocery list. She also checks the newspaper for specials. Depending on what they are, she makes her menus accordingly.

In planning ahead, Ruth limits her shopping to one trip weekly. She's able to provide a balanced diet for the family.

She's also able to include the proper nutrients. This often is lacking when the homemaker fixes foods on impulse, on the spur-of-the-moment, with whatever she happens to have on hand. I would suggest, however, that you do use leftovers. They may be incorporated in another dish, or served separately. One family member may be glad for extra food!

One home economist says you meet the basic nutrient requirements if daily you serve one yellow and one green vegetable, one egg per person (may be used in custards, cakes, or puddings), a pint of milk for each adult and a quart per child, one meat (or other protein foods), grain foods, milk products, and some fats and carbohydrates and fruits.

Limit sweets and desserts for growing children until after they have eaten vegetables, meat, and fruit.

Remember—a balanced meal is colorful.


## Family Involved

The family will enjoy eating together the tasty meals you've prepared and served attractively. Enlist the children's cooperation in preparing the food, in setting an attractive table, in cleaning up afterwards. These all belong to "family"—to building good relationships—to unity and harmony.

When possible, eat leisurely. Encourage family conversation, sharing the highlights of the day and reporting fun and surprises. Around our table we often shared current jokes. As the children get older they share issues of the day, their plans, and desires.

Family table talk plays an important part in the lives of many parents and children. Try to make it profitable and interesting.

## NUTRIENTS

In meal planning you'll need to consider the nutrients a body needs—proteins, minerals (especially calcium and iron), vitamins, and carbohydrates.

Proteins are essential to build healthy bodies. Animal sources of protein are milk products, eggs, fish, poultry, and meat. Vegetable sources are dried beans, peas, cereals, breads, peanut butter.

Minerals help regulate the body as well as build it. As you choose foods rich in iron and calcium, you'll also have the dozen other necessary minerals. Milk is the best source of calcium. The next best source is greens.

The chief source of iron is liver—also available in lean meats, dried fruit (uncooked), molasses, some vegetables, whole grain cereals.

There are some twenty vitamins, but watching Vitamins A, B, C, D will give you all you need.

Vitamin A is found in whole milk and milk foods, liver, egg yolks, vegetables (both green and yellow).

Vitamin B has its source in muscle meats (liver, kidney, heart), legumes, egg yolks, and whole grains.

Vitamin C is found in citrus fruits, tomatoes, uncooked cabbage, cantaloupes, broccoli, brussels sprouts, and potatoes (if regularly eaten).

Vitamin D comes from milk, fish oils, egg yolk, and liver.

Carbohydrates (starch and sugar) and fats are necessary sources of energy.

You'll want to include these sources of nutrients in your daily menus.

## MARKETING KNOWLEDGE

The creative cook considers the family's likes and dislikes. She *wants* to please them. At the same time she is careful to include nutritious dishes. She needs to know the kind of nutrients which build the body. She takes off from there as she plans menus and does her marketing.

Careful meal planning and shopping calls for experience in marketing. What are the best buys? (Not that you buy only cheap foods, but you will want to buy the best in basic nourishing foods, and keep within your budget.)

This requires time daily, and many hours each week. You can resent it—or enjoy it as a necessary part to creating dishes the family enjoys. It's well to remember to buy foods in season. Watch sales on canned goods when the new season is close at hand.

Learning to use different seasonings and experimenting with each helps make cooking an enjoyable art. So does trying new recipes.

Here's a not-too-well-known recipe. Why not experiment with it?

### Green Tomato Pie

3 cups green sliced tomatoes (unpeeled)
1 tablespoon lemon juice
1 teaspoon grated lemon rind
¾ cup sugar
1 tablespoon butter
1 tablespoon cornstarch

Mix ingredients together. Bring to boil. Pour into unbaked pie crust and bake 30 minutes in 350° F. oven. It's delicious!

### FUN AND ENJOYMENT

Preparing tasty nutritious foods and experimenting with baking breads, cakes, pies, and other pastry help fill the creative urge within every homemaker. For many homemakers these are very natural outlets for experiencing satisfaction and fulfillment as a homemaker. Your rewards are the family's enjoyment, appreciation, and healthy bodies.

The smells coming from the kitchen are very deep in a child's memories—those teasing odors like breads, cakes, cinnamon buns, roast chicken, ham. Not only do they influence growing children, but even adults. Just recently our married daughter and husband stepped into our house. The aroma of roast beef and fresh vegetables cooking greeted them. Both of them hurried to the kitchen exclaiming, "Mom, that smell. It's great!" If they said it once, they said it five times. And really meant it.

I accepted their enthusiastic compliments with a sense of satisfaction and fulfillment, happy to be able to prepare a meal they enjoy.

Unfortunately many a homemaker doesn't enjoy cooking. It's a burden. Another chore. She views it in disgust —probably as a result of never having experienced preparing meals. Then suddenly she's confronted with cooking. Three meals daily, seven days a week, four weeks a month, twelve months per year is more than she can cope with.

Cooking is an art that every homemaker can enjoy as she employs her heart, and hands, and mind—as well as proper ingredients and tested recipes.

## Outdoor Meals

Eating outdoors on trays is a fine solution to the youngsters' cries, "Let's eat out," when you're up to your neck with cleaning, painting, sewing, or just returned from an appointment or activity.

For this you prepare the meal as planned. The children fill their own plates and carry them (on a tray) to a shady spot on the lawn.

This can also be a form of entertaining. The older child can help you fix the guests' trays or serve them individually seated on the lawn.

You may frequently use the outdoor fireplace or the grill for meals out. It's best to prepare the fire twenty or thirty minutes prior to needing it. Let it burn down to live coals. This is a much better heat than a blazing one.

For something different to serve, prepare your hamburger for meat loaf. Then press into patties and cook over the outdoor fire. Delicious! Another change is to prepare a one-kettle meal outside—stew, meatballs and spaghetti.

An easy sauce to fix, and tasty, for your barbecue steaks, chicken or pork chops is this one: Mix together thoroughly equal portions of vinegar, cooking oil, tomato juice seasoned with salt, sugar, minced garlic, onions, and parsley. Yummy!

Picnics are in order during the warm season. Take your salads, fresh vegetables, and meats in the cooler. Prepare plenty of drinks and finger foods. Make a list of all you need—food, materials to fix fire, napkins, drink, washcloth, can opener, cups, plates, and bag for garbage. And don't forget to check off each item as you pack.

Be creative in your outdoor cooking. The family will love you for it.

## WITH LOVE

Creative cooking can be fun and enjoyable, as you stir lots of love into your meals. Try it!

> Once upon a time I planned to be
> An artist of celebrity.
> A song I thought to write one day,
> And all the world would homage pay.

I longed to write a noted book
  But what I did was—learn to cook.
For life with simple tasks is filled,
  And I have done, not what I willed,
Yet when I see boys' hungry eyes
  I'm glad I make good apple pies!

ELIZABETH THOMAS

# 7

# Food Preservation

Food prices have been rising!

Dr. Don Paarlberg, top economist, U.S. Department of Agriculture, predicts an increase in processed fruits and vegetables. Because production costs increased last year "these factors probably will be reflected in higher prices for canned and frozen fruits and vegetables," he says in a *U.S. News and World Report* article.

## AVOID SPOILAGE

In light of high costs, preserve food carefully during the hot summer months. You'll need to be extra cautious in food storage to avoid spoilage. You can't afford to waste food.

Clear food away immediately from the table, or on picnics. Place leftovers immediately in the refrigerator, or in the cooler you've taken along. If you pack your husband's lunch, remember mayonnaise spoils fast and his lunch may be on the hot truck seat all forenoon. Here's an idea: Use frozen bread for his sandwich or make sandwich ahead of time and freeze. This will keep it cool for a longer time.

## PRESERVING FOR WINTER USE

Many homemakers pay today's high prices and think nothing of it. But others have taken a different approach. Some have gone back to gardening. Others are trying it as a first-time adventure. They want to be sure they have enough to eat this summer and some for winter use.

Many homemakers who don't have gardens load up the children and enjoy driving to the country to buy fresh vegetables or fruit by the bushel; or they get the food for nothing because a farmer has more than his family can use. He's only too glad for someone to pick the vegetables or fruits and use them.

## COMMUNITY GARDEN

I was delighted to read recently in the *Reader's Digest* ("Fresh Food for the Picking" by James G. Driscoll) how one Wisconsin man, a pastor, thought up and organized a community garden project. The fresh food was available for the picking. It attracted 259 families in 1972 and over 2,000 the next year.

The main factor in its success is that someone else does 90 percent of the hard work, by machinery. The families themselves weed little but harvest a lot. Lionel Harold (the owner of the farm where the original gardens began) plows, prepares the soil and plants seeds. The section covers thirteen acres. Later he divides the area into 1,000 square-foot family plots. Each plot has a private access strip for parking, weeding, and harvesting. The owner charges each family ten dollars to cover cost of seeds and plants bought in bulk, rent, and labor. Harold (the owner) and garden managers get two dollars an hour. From this small investment a family picks close to three hundred dollars' worth of fresh fruit and vegetables all summer. Much of it they freeze for winter eating.

What a splendid idea to help families who are trying to combat spiraling food costs!

## Food Is Available

If you drive to the country for your fresh food, occasionally make it a time of fun as well as work. Take a picnic lunch along—to eat at the roadside park, or in a meadow or under a shady tree.

After you return home with the produce, prepare it immediately. Prompt and careful handling means much in retaining fresh flavor, texture, and nutrient value. Select only the best foods.

You may gather wild asparagus that grows along the roadside. That's always a welcome early vegetable. It's good for freezing, too.

Perhaps you also pick wild berries. It's a very simple method to freeze the extra ones you're unable to eat now.

You may hesitate to preserve food. It's hard work. On the other hand, it can be a lovely family project. When you think of the 800 million who are malnourished according to a recent United Nations report, thank God that food is available. Also thank Him for the health and mental ability to prepare sufficient food for your family.

You may not be able to preserve foods in quantity, but you can utilize the freezer part in your refrigerator to store the special sale items.

## Fun While Working

This requires work. That's why you want to involve the children. Often husband can help, too, after he comes home from his job. The old adage applies here: MANY HANDS MAKE LIGHT WORK.

Make it a pleasant time. Initiate some games. With

younger children involved, play "I'm thinking of a color." The one who's "it" selects a colored item, keeping it a secret. The others are to guess the color. The one guessing it then becomes "it."

This situation is an excellent time to sing together, to memorize Scripture, and repeat verses already learned. It's a time to discuss family experiences and share together.

At our house we often used this time to create stories. One began with a short paragraph and each took his/her turn to add to the story. We'd almost crack up at some of the weird tales concocted! While shelling peas, we vied with each other to see which one had the pod with the most peas. All the time the work was getting done—and we were having fun.

The working mother will not have time for a lot of food conserving, but there are after-work hours or Saturdays when she can plan for family involvement in such a project.

## CHILDREN LIKE VEGETABLES

One mother responds, "But my children won't eat fresh vegetables, especially not greens!"

Authorities indicate that it's easy to get your child to eat vegetables. Studies conducted at the University of New Mexico on children ages five-and-a-half to seven-and-a-half verify this. Before lunch, one group watched a child who served as a model eating the greens and enjoying them. The other groups saw no model. The children who watched the model ate more greens than the others.

So, mother, you know what to do to get your child to eat fresh vegetables—invite someone over to eat the vegetables with gusto!

## FREEZING

Modern food freezing is a result of man's efforts for many years to find a way to preserve foods without changing their flavors, colors, or textures.

It's great to be able to have at your fingertips a supply of fresh vegetables, fruits, meats, baked goods, and dairy products.

Research shows that freezing retains the health-giving vitamins and minerals better than any other food preservation method.

You needn't fear botulin in frozen foods. Freezing checks the physical action of microorganisms that cause food spoilage. Be sure to follow the instructions which accompany your freezer.

Use moisture and vapor-proof packaging and wrapping materials to wrap the food. This is a protection from the cold, dry freezer air. Wrap food in portions according to the size of your family.

Preserve foods when they are in season and are abundant. This means lower prices and high quality.

Don't keep food longer than from one season to the next. Bacon and seasoned sausage need to be used within six months. The salt accelerates the development of rancidity in fat meats. All pork should be used quickly. Baked goods, too, should be used within months.

Freeze only the foods your family enjoys. Many homemakers keep a list of foods in the freezer and check off items as they use them. This makes it easy to plan your meals. It reminds you of food that might otherwise be stored too long.

## Preparation

In freezing vegetables—wash them, cut into desired lengths, blanch about three minutes in boiling water. Drain. Cool thoroughly. Drain and place in airtight containers allowing one-half inch at the top for expansion.

For freezing fruits: Wash fruit, cut in desired pieces, place in containers, add sugar, and seal. Consult proper guides for the different types of foods.

I frequently use jars that I've collected through the year —jam, peanut butter, small mayonnaise, pint coffee jars. Leave room for expansion and seal tightly. One caution —when you use the glass jars, be careful when you thaw them. Set them out to thaw in room temperature, not under the hot water faucet.

## Canning

Some homemakers prefer canning certain fruits and vegetables to freezing them. You'll need to know the proper use of canning equipment. Carefully follow instructions which come with the pressure cooker or canner. Acquaint yourself thoroughly with processing and cooling techniques. Choose standard jars and caps which properly fit the jar. This insures an airtight seal—which is a *must* in canning.

It's well to consult someone experienced in canning as well as the local home economist either at the school, county, or state Extension Service. They'll be happy to help you in this creative and profitable venture.

You can use hot water bath, pressure cooker, cold or hot pack method. Fruit keeps well when canned from an open kettle. Be sure the fruit is boiling hot and has sufficient sugar. Fill the sterilized hot jars and tightly seal.

## CREATIVE WORK

If you're in for real adventure, try pickling cucumbers. It's lots of fun, and you'll enjoy the tasty pickles next winter. Relish can be made from combining the last of the garden vegetables.

Store canned foods in a cool room—possibly in your basement or garage. Arrange them neatly on the shelves.

The wise man Solomon advises: "It's better to work, even get your hands dirty—and have enough to eat than to expect everything to come your way—with little or no effort on your part" (*see* Proverbs 12:9).

The family has to eat. So take advantage, homemaker, of the fruits and vegetables when they are available at a lower cost to you.

You'll be proud of your creative work, resulting in nutritious food, easily available in the winter months to feed your family—and to share with someone in need.

# 8

# Laundry and Clothes Care

Someone has said, "The best things are nearest: breath in your nostrils, light in your eyes, flowers at your feet, duties at your hand, the path of God just before you. Then do not grasp at the stars, but do life's common tasks as they come . . . daily duties and daily bread are among the sweetest things of life."

Daily duties can be sweet (including the laundry), when we are ever mindful that it is one segment in preparing useful, happy citizens—both for this world and for the world to come.

## LAUNDRY TODAY

Washday is a far cry from what it used to be—hand wringer, boiling clothes, washboard. Now it's sort clothes, place in washer, push buttons, and go about your other duties!

The location of the home laundry has changed drastically from days of old. It's no longer an old shed, dark basement, or back porch. In today's new homes, the automatic washer and dryer now find a place in the kitchen or utility room nearby. Some are located close to the bedroom, since four-fifths of the laundry comes from the bedroom area.

## Laundry of Yesteryear

I remember washday as a young girl. We pumped water by hand to fill the large iron kettle. Carried in wood and built a fire under the kettle. Sorted the clothes. When the water boiled, we cautiously dipped it into the washing machine, added chipped homemade soap, put in the clothes, and started the motor. After the desired length of washing was completed, the white clothes were transferred to the kettle of boiling water—stomped with a tin clothes stomper, put through the wringer, and then rinsed through two tubs of water. The other clothes went straight to the rinse water from the machine.

Halfway through the laundry process, we emptied the first tub of rinse water, carrying the buckets of water to water the flowers, vegetables, and fruit trees. Then we transferred the second tubful of water into the first tub and filled the second tub with fresh water. Get it? Quite a process! But there were enough boys and girls to do all this work. We took turns. No one was overworked.

But that's not all. After all the clothes were washed, we emptied all the tubs, carrying the water outside when the weather allowed. In cold weather we poured it down a floor drain.

The clothes were wrung into a reed basket, which we placed in the little red wagon, and pulled it under the clothes line. Every piece was hung outside to dry in the sunshine and fresh air.

Quite a procedure! Now we wash clothes as a sideline, usually drying them in a dryer.

## White Laundry

To keep white clothes white, we need to use some kind of bleach. Without the natural bleach of sunshine (and boiling water) this substitute is necessary.

I discovered in Argentina that white clothes remained white without commercial bleach or hot water. This was the procedure: The laundress would wet the article in cold water and rub it generously with a piece of dark laundry soap. She then spread the wet-soaped articles of clothing on a large piece of tin, or on the green grass in the bright sun. After several hours she rubbed the garments in cold water, using a corrugated washboard, rinsed them carefully, and hung them in the sun to dry. The white clothes were pure white. The colored clothes were sudsed and rubbed in cold water, but not exposed to the sun treatment.

For the first years in Argentina when I was without a washing machine or laundress, I'd put the dirty clothes in the bathtub, add flaked soap and cover them with hot water, and let them soak overnight. The next day they required very little hand rubbing, if any. I'd wring out the soapy water and rinse several times in fresh water. Then hang them out to dry. They got nice and clean.

I'm glad those laundry days are past!

## Your Laundry Needs

What are your laundry needs? How can you meet them? What are the expenses involved? Can you meet the costs?

If you frequent a self-service laundry thinking that it is cheaper, here are some interesting comparisons. Some market research figures reveal that the cost of a home-owned washing unit is fourteen to twenty cents a load, whereas, in a coin-operated laundry you pay twenty-five or thirty cents per load. According to these figures (assuming the washer costs $225, guaranteed for ten years, $52 service and upkeep cost and 7.1 loads per week), you will save enough from your home unit to replace your machine "free" every four years.

You may have no choice but to use a nearby laundromat. You'll need to know which is for you.

If you plan to do your own laundry at home, you may choose a wringer-type washer. You'll need two tubs, filter hose, and adequate clothes lines.

With an automatic washer, you eliminate the tubs and hose. You'll need very little clothes line if you also have a dryer. Other equipment includes iron, ironing board, cabinet or table for stain removal kit, detergents, and soaps. If you iron your linens and sheets, you may want an ironer, and a chair to sit on while ironing.

More and more women feel that automatic washers are a necessity, not a luxury. The main reason is—it saves time. Whenever I hear that, immediately I question, "Saves time for what?"

Home economists say automatic washers do *not* do a better job of getting clothes clean. They require more hot water than the wringer-type washer. There are more breakdowns because of their delicate parts. For many homemakers, the expenses involved keep this machine from their homes. In some locations lack of water supply eliminates the automatic washer.

## Preparing to Wash

Your laundry arrangement requires four centers: sorting, washing, drying, and ironing. At each center you'll want to assemble the necessary equipment.

For best results, sort similar clothes to be washed together—white clothes—fast-colored pastels and linens

—fabrics requiring special handling, such as woolens, nylons, nonfast colored cottons—wash-and-wear clothes and rayons—finally dark, heavy work clothes.

When you sort clothes, check all the pockets, and remove anything in them. Close zippers, so they won't get ruined. Also check for stains. Some stains you may need to spot clean, for washing sets them. I've discovered that a "degreaser" solution rubbed on soiled neckbands and shirt cuffs and greasy jeans before putting them in the machine does the job marvelously.

For a homemade degreaser rub pure lard on the grease spots. Wait for thirty minutes, then wash in hot sudsy water.

Don't overload your machine. This turns out a poor wash. If you have hard water, use water softener with your soap powder or detergent.

If there is no determined cycle on your machine wash fragile things several minutes. Heavily soiled garments require ten to fifteen minutes. Linens, bedding, shirts need about half that length of time.

Read carefully the labels attached to clothing, and follow directions for laundry.

## DRYING

If you use a roller wringer, remember to fold the clothes neatly before feeding into wringer. The bulk should be evenly distributed to prevent clogging the wringer. Clothes with large buttons or buckles should be wrung out by hand. Fold small buttons or zippers under a layer of fabric and feed in flat. Several small articles can be fed through together. Don't force or pull on clothes. Let the machine wring at its own pace.

If you use an automatic dryer, don't overdry. Some moisture in the fabric makes textures softer and fluffier.

I don't pose as a fresh-air fiend, but I'm aware of the important place fresh air and sunshine have in keeping healthy. I love to hang clothes outside. To smell their fresh fragrance, especially when I crawl between the sheets after a weary day, is just one of my many rewards as a home-maker. Frankly, I don't like the blah odor of clothes dried in automatic dryers, even though I use one quite frequently.

Bacteriologists claim that drying garments in the sun and air kills any bacteria in the garments. Hanging up the clothes and gathering them again also affords an opportunity for exercise outdoors. This every housewife needs.

Hang the clothes properly. This eliminates a lot of ironing and makes the ironing easier. Hang sheets evenly over the line. Shake out each garment. Hang shirts by their tails. Hang dresses by hems from side seams, or straight of cloth. This avoids sagging. Some dresses you may want to hang on hangers. Hang skirts and trousers by the waistband, or a hanger. Colored clothes should be hung in the shade or indoors.

Never wring water out of corduroys, velveteens or woolens. This ruins the fibers and shape of the garment. Gently squeeze and lay on heavy towels to dry.

## IRONING

I have a friend who declares ironing was her most-hated job. She would let it pile up and iron only when absolutely necessary. But several years ago something happened. She learned to love Jesus Christ, and relate closely to Him. He gave her a new joy. Today she irons beautifully and frequently irons for others to earn a bit of extra spending money. She didn't write the following poem, but could have:

# 9

# Limit Your Budget

"If only we had more money, then I'd be happy!" Have you ever said that? or at least thought it?

But the statement just isn't true! Money is not the source of happiness. True, no one can live without it. It's a necessary item of exchange, but the best things of life are still free.

The Greek actress, Melina Mercouri, warns young girls that money isn't everything, and possessions can be a danger. She insists, "Beyond a few comforts, money doesn't change your life or solve problems. After all, you can only wear one dress at a time."

Concerning possessions she confesses, "I hesitate to buy things because they frequently make a slave of me. One cannot dance through life freely when one is weighted down."

I don't know how many dresses Melina owns, or what all she possesses. Being an actress she probably lacks nothing, but I do agree with her philosophy. And from her vantage point she can speak authoritatively on the subject.

## DECEITFUL

Money talks. Money allows you to get things. You don't need to depend on anyone else, not even God. But money is illusive. Those who put their trust in riches will some day be deceived. Money is no guarantee of security. One day you have it. The next day it may be gone. And then, what will you have in life?

Someone wisely stated: "Money is a universal passport to everywhere, except heaven, and is a provider of everything but happiness."

### Money Will Buy

A bed but not sleep.
Books but not brains.
Food but not appetite.
Finery but not beauty.
A house but not a home.
Medicine but not health.
Luxuries but not culture.
Amusements but not happiness.
Religion but not salvation.

## CAUSES OF MARRIAGE PROBLEMS

Marriage counselors rate money high in the causes of a couple's quarrels. When the couple sets up housekeeping they're carried away by adventure and abundance of things. They also want to have the best, at least as nice as their parents have. They forget how many years it's taken their parents to arrive at where they are—forget that for many years they did without many so-called necessities. The couple's energy and time and effort is put into earning money and not enough thought to learning to live together.

Money is a chief cause of divorce. One partner spends thoughtlessly; or the husband refuses to consult with his wife on financial matters. Their differences have never been resolved, are always a source of irritation. So they decide to separate.

In reality, there are deep personality problems, but money problems increase their seriousness.

## Too Much Money

I think one of the greatest tragedies of today is our wealth—the ease with which it's gotten. People no longer work for a job, only for money.

In spite of the fact that per capita earnings have hit an all-time high in history, almost everyone grumbles about being underpaid—the day laborer, the public schoolteacher, college professors, even the preachers.

Money just doesn't reach. As a young bride stated: "Boy, how I need help. We are beyond ourselves in debt. It happened so gradually we didn't realize we were being ensnared like many other couples. We'd appreciate any help you could give us along that line."

A "Heart to Heart" listener wrote asking for help "on balancing the budget. I believe the art of spending money wisely is as important as learning how to earn it." She is so right!

Money can be a medium of exchange for the necessities of life or it can be your master, controlling your life.

## Lack Training

Personal bankruptcy, which has increased greatly the past decade, is not due to unemployment, substandard income, sickness, or any major family misfortune. According to a life-insurance report the number one cause is mismanagement of family income.

There are many reasons for a couple's overspending, but

I'd like to suggest one reason, especially from the wife's angle: lack of training in how to spend.

Margaret writes, "I am a young housewife and mother and have never had much training in marketing . . . My problem is not knowing how to shop and make the most of money that is alloted for groceries. I try to buy only what's necessary with the money our budget allows. Most of our meals leave some of the family still hungry . . . I am more than willing to learn."

## CREDIT BUYING

Another reason for too-big a debt is credit buying.

"Easy credit" drives more families to financial failure each year.

"We figure that five or six of every 100 American families are in serious financial trouble," says Robert Gibson, president of the National Foundation for Consumer Credit in a *U.S. News and World Report* article.

The problem is people have never learned how to use credit. Some families use their credit cards when their money doesn't hold out—forgetting they need to pay some day—usually at 18 percent annual interest.

## EXCESSIVE SPENDING

Many families' debts arise from the area of excessive spending—for bigger and better models, expensive restaurants, expensive gifts. They buy the biggest and newest —partly from being brainwashed by modern advertising —partly in an effort to keep up with the Joneses. An excessive money leak for some women is the hairdresser or cosmetics. For men, it's expensive hobbies, or pastimes —such as sports-car driving, photography, boating, or too frequent bowling.

## How Get Out of Debt?

An authority on finance gives advice on how to get out, and stay out of debt. Among his many good practical ideas was the surprising one: *"Work out a hardcore budget and stick to it."* He says stick to the basic expenses—food, clothing, housing, medical care, which come first. As you do this you'll be amazed at the large amount of nonessential spending you've been doing.

Author Charlie W. Shedd believes you should live on a self-denying budget. It's who you are, not what you have that figures. "More important than the house you live in is what kind of you is living in the house!" he writes in *Letters to Karen*. The kind of sofa is less important than what you share in visiting, dreaming, and planning as you sit on the sofa.

Through a limited budget the Shedds learned some invaluable secrets. They lived by this money motto: *Give ten percent, save ten percent, and spend the rest with thanksgiving and praise!*

## Planned Spending

In "How to Stretch Your Money," Sidney Margolius, noted authority on family economics, advises planned spending rather than strict budgeting. To arrive at such a plan you'll have to keep track of expenses for a year, total the amount spent in a given area, and divide by twelve to obtain a monthly spending. Then determine the percentage for the different areas: food, clothing, medicines, and so forth. Also allow a small account for both you and your husband to spend with no asking.

He warns not to be persuaded to have others manage your money, with credits, or quick loans. Although it's very simple to get into debt this way, "No one has invented a simple way to get out."

Some major items have to be bought on credit—house, car, or appliances, but go slow on credit buying. Know the costs of installment credit and borrowed money. Credit unions' rates range from 8 to 12 percent and licensed small loan companies charge from 8 to 42 percent depending on the purpose of the loan.

To arrive at the amount for an outstanding debt, principal and interest included, take 10 percent of your monthly take-home pay, multiply by 19; or, from your annual take-home pay subtract annual payments for shelter, food, tax, insurance, and so forth, and divide by 3.

Margolius suggests plugging leaks in these areas of spending: food, insurance, commercial entertainment, transportation costs, and household upkeep.

Watch out for door-to-door salesmen. Don't sign quickly on the dotted lines, for they often pressure you too quickly and don't reveal all involved.

Learn to save a percentage of your net income. Also put aside at least a tenth for giving to the church, charity, missions. Don't shortchange God. After all He who owns everything, has only loaned it to you for your use.

## Ways to Economize

There are positive ways to economize. Take advantage of food specials.

Know your product—its quality—and compare prices.

Buy during seasonable sales at reliable stores.

Get over the idea that everything you buy has to be brand-new. Secondhand furniture, for example, is a good investment for young couples—especially if you'll be moving soon.

Do without some items for the time being.

Spend less for certain items, like a spring coat. Cut down on entertainment and nonessentials.

Use your own skills instead of paying for services—make the café curtains you wanted instead of buying them; wash your own car; refinish the furniture.

Pack your lunch instead of buying it.

Take advantage of free community services for education and recreation—concerts, parks, libraries, lectures, recreational centers, art exhibits—rather than patronize paid entertainments.

Earn pin money without taking a job outside the home, if you feel your place is at home with the children. One mother bakes wedding cakes and helps plan the wedding. Another takes in sewing. Another bakes breads and pies to sell; or a part-time job allowing you to still meet the family's needs, may be your answer.

## BASIC ATTITUDES

Your basic attitudes toward money and the things it buys largely determine how you live—within a budget based on your income (whether one or both partners work) or constantly dodging creditors.

*How much* money you have is not your solution. Remember, money is deceitful. Don't set your heart on it. "The love of money is the root of all evil" says the Good Book (1 Timothy 6:10). God owns everything. He only loans you these temporal gifts. You are a steward—one who takes care of what's entrusted to him/her. He demands faithful stewardship.

Another attitude is to clarify your wants and needs. If you don't, modern advertising will. Radio, TV, newspapers, and magazines bombard you on every side to buy this and that.

Their goal is to convince you that what you have you don't want, or isn't good enough. Don't you believe them. Ask God to help you sort out your wants from needs.

## CONTENTMENT

A basic attitude is to make the most of what you have and don't focus on what you don't have. Learn to be content with what you have. Your life doesn't consist of your possessions. Life consists of relationships—both to God and others—of feelings and emotions, of goals, of adventure, of accomplishments, of obedience to God, and faithfulness to Him and to each other.

A wife needs to express appreciation to her husband for his efforts to provide. She needs to encourage him in his job. Let him know his long hours and routine work aren't in vain. Many men have reached the point of "I don't care." They do their best but can't satisfy a demanding wife. A husband is more apt to enjoy his job and work all the harder when he knows she thinks he's the greatest. This attitude helps to bring him straight home after work.

## A JOINT VENTURE

Dr. Charlie W. Shedd suggests that a husband should have a major amount of say in how the money should be spent. A wife may be the better financier of the two. However, if you are to manage the budget, let it be his decision for you to do it. I've seen ruined marriages simply because the wife took over of her own accord, and completely—leaving no area of financial responsibility to her husband.

Regardless of who assumes responsibility for writing checks and paying bills it should be a joint venture. You'll want to consult together about beyond-regular-budget spending. As in all other areas, you need honesty and frankness about personal feelings, about your desires and needs. Remember, it's up to you to control the money, not allow money to control you.

## MONEY A BLESSING

Make money your servant, and not your master. This is possible as you define your goals and priorities. As you choose proper attitudes toward money and toward the things money can buy. As you take God in as your partner.

This includes a carefully arranged budget which may mean some self-denial and sacrificing of frills. It means sorting out needs from mere wants—focusing on the outlets rather than the intake—returning to God His share (at least a tenth)—laying up treasures in heaven as you give to those in need —trusting God when funds are low, or not there. He has promised to supply all your needs through Jesus Christ our Lord. (*See* Philippians 4:19.) When you do His will, and are eager to follow His "rightness," all the necessities of life will be supplied to you. (*See* Matthew 6:33.)

Using money as a blessing to others, and to God, brings contentment and happiness to you.

# 10

# Home Safety

Home is where the harm is, according to some authorities.

There were 4,250,000 home and accidental injuries in 1972. From these 27,000 deaths resulted. 110,000 were permanently impaired, according to the 1974 *World Almanac and Book of Facts*.

In 1970, 9,600 persons of all ages died as a result of falls, cites a *Parents Magazine* article on safety. They tripped over shoes, toys and other objects left in the middle of the room, over furniture moved from its usual place, over loose carpets. Some fell down stairs. Others slipped on spilled food or waxed floors.

## FAMILY STRAIN

I was much interested in the study at the Children's Hospital in Boston (1963). Dr. Roger J. Meyer discovered that most children's accidents are the result of strain in the family. And wouldn't you know—in most cases strain directly involving Mother! In 1900, fatalities among children as a result of accidents was fifth, today they rank first. In the Boston findings, accidents occur most frequently (1) during the hour before a meal; (2) when mother is ill, (3) when

95

children are in the care of persons unfamiliar with their routine, (4) when other family members are ill, or are the center of mother's attention; (5) when relationship of parents is tense; (6) when the environment of the child is about to be changed.

Dr. Meyer's team was surprised at the apparent ignorance of even educated parents. Less than 50 percent realized the severity of the injury at the time it happened. Most of the group didn't even know that aspirin was a poison.

The researchers are trying to find a foolproof way to isolate the factors responsible for the fatalities. They even suggest giving shots against some accidents!

## SAFETY IN THE KITCHEN

Did you know that nearly one-fourth of all home accidents occur in the kitchen? That's one room we couldn't possibly get along without. We do need the kitchen, but we must also be aware of safety precautions. You need the stove, but if there are small children in your home, you should consider a stove with switches out of their reach. If that's impossible, here's one area where you need to enforce obedience.

Only a few months ago I read about a child's death caused by severe burns. He had pulled a kettle of hot water over him. Remember to turn pot handles so that neither you nor the youngsters will accidentally upset them.

I was made conscious recently that synthetic clothing materials are more hazardous than other kinds. A young mother was warming the baby's bottle. She lifted the pan off the gas burner and reached across the burner to place it on the other side. Her ruffled nylon pajama sleeve instantly caught fire. The blaze swept up her arm and across her back. She spent several weeks recovering in the hospital.

## Prevention

It's imperative for parents and other members of the family to learn how to prevent accidents to children. Infants need absolute protection, and should never be left alone —even for a moment on a bathinette. Safety belts should be used on the bathinette.

The crib bars must be close together so the head will not become caught. When children begin to toddle, safety gates should be placed at top and bottom of stairs and on porches.

Begin a safety campaign right now. Use preventive measures. Enlist the children's cooperation. Keep stairsteps clean, free from toys and other articles. Clear out the piles of trash and paper next to the furnace. Turn handles of pots and pans on the stove inward. Lock the medicine chest. Keep detergents, sprays, insecticides, furniture polish, and sharp instruments out of Jacky's reach.

## Summer Hurts

Summertime brings more than the usual hurts and pains. The children play out-of-doors, and if barefoot, often step on nails, broken glass, or even bees. They may also climb trees, fences, old buildings, and what have you!

Granted, accidents are bound to happen, but we will also want to make the yard a safe place for children to play in. We should clean up rubbish, keep trash in containers and avoid accidents as much as possible. Sharp tools should not be allowed to lie around. As parents we'll set the example in placing the hedge clippers, saw, and ax out of their reach.

The rotary mower has proved to be quite dangerous. I think we parents shouldn't allow small youngsters to use it. When he is old enough to use the mower, the child should be taught never to remove sticks or foreign articles while the motor is running. He should be cautious as to where he uses the mower. An uneven terrace or stony area may prove dangerous.

There are thousands of lawn mower injuries every year in the USA. Running a power mower is no job for young children. Only a person with good judgment and a familiarity with the mower should operate it. And for you who do use it, wear sturdy shoes. This may save a toe. Pick up all stones and sharp objects before you mow.

## FIREPROOF HOMES?

Some of us haven't been choosers when it came to selecting materials in the home in which we live at the present. Possibly fiberboards with combustible surfaces were used for interior walls. But if you are about to build, it would be worth investigating fiberboard, finished plywoods, or doors that have been factory-treated with fire-retarding chemicals.

For acoustical and plastic tile which have had flame-spread characteristics, flame-proof sprays or surface coatings are the only safeguard.

High, narrow windows have prevented many people from escaping in case of emergencies. The popular one-door house is a hazard in the ultramodern home.

You'll want to think through just what action you should take, and your best means of escape, in case of a fire in your home.

It's true, we can't build 100 percent fireproof homes. We'll do what's possible, and at the same time ask God to protect us.

## POISONOUS ITEMS

The common cause of poisoning no longer is food. About 50 percent of children's deaths are caused by drugs or medicaments.

Drinking kerosene and other petroleum products account for about one fourth of deaths of children under five years. Other fatalities occur from lead poisoning as well as toilet-bowl cleansers, oven cleaners, and other items found in most homes.

In every home there are many household products which contain one or more toxic ingredients. Included in these products are: hair spray, detergents, DDT, insect sprays, bleaches, furniture polish, barbiturates, tranquilizers, aspirin, alcohol, kerosene, lye, moth balls, and boric acid. The National Clearing House for Poison Control Centers in Washington, D.C., has in its files the brand names of several thousand of these products.

Another poison is the castor bean. Many grow these on lawns in an attempt to prevent mole damage. Both the leaf and bean are dangerous. Four to six beans could be a lethal dose.

Polystyrene plastic cement sniffed by some teen-agers for "kicks" can be dangerous. A famous toxicologist warns that this may permanently damage the liver and bone marrow which replenishes the body's blood supply.

## Most Common Causes

You might be surprised to know that the children most commonly brought to poison-control centers are those who have swallowed furniture polish. Some brands contain petroleum. Some don't. And each kind calls for a different treatment. First-aid directions are on the label.

Swallowing an overdose of baby aspirin (the colored and sweetened kind) is the leading cause of accidental deaths among young children, reports Dr. Louis W. Sauer.

How did the child get the aspirins? One mother let the

child play with the bottle. When she returned to the crib an hour later, the child had chewed off the plastic lid.

In another case a three-year-old boy and his sister found the aspirin bottle on the sink. In one serious episode the mother failed to put the lid back on the bottle after giving a tablet to the baby.

Dr. Sauer's advice for mothers is that they should make their watchword "think ahead of time."

I recall an incident when one of our sons, about four years old, swallowed a moth ball. Since there were no harmful results, it's rather amusing now. I was confined in the hospital. My sister who was caring for the boys immediately informed my husband. To induce vomiting they decided to feed him castor oil (which would have caused either one of them to vomit). Nothing happened after the first spoonful. So they gave him another and another. And to their astonishment the little fellow wanted more. "It tastes like jelly!" he said.

With their purpose foiled, his daddy carried him to the bathroom, turned him upside down, and placed his finger down his throat. Well, that took care of both the castor oil and the moth ball!

(We never did discover where he found that moth ball.)

## PRECAUTIONS

This word of caution is applicable for any product: BE SURE TO READ THE LABEL! And anything that is poisonous keep out of the child's reach. *Please!* "An ounce of prevention is worth a pound of cure!"

Bubble-bath containers which are used as toys should first be emptied and thoroughly cleansed. The product can cause serious skin irritation. Go through your medicine cabinet periodically and discard old medications—don't keep left-over drugs from a past illness unless on doctor's advice. Discard any preparation that has changed color consistency or become cloudy—especially old iodine, eye and most nose drops, cough remedies, and ointments.

Even if you think you have taught Jacky not to play under the kitchen sink (where you likely store detergents, polish, insecticides), there will inevitably come the time when he is alone, or alone with some playmates, and he will begin to explore. In some way, you'll need to securely fasten the door, or never leave the child alone. Take extra precautions for his safety.

A sweet little two-year-old boy swallowed lye one day while his mother was hanging up clothes. He was rushed to the hospital, but this quick-acting poison had done it's work—eaten part of his esophagus and stomach. He was hospitalized for weeks. Finally he was able to come home, but with an inserted tube. He will carry this handicap throughout life.

In case of poisoning, immediately call the doctor, tell what the suspected poison is, then carefully obey his orders. A local pediatrician recommends having a bottle of ipecac in your medicine cabinet to induce vomiting in order to empty the child's stomach immediately. You can also give the child egg whites, cream, or tepid water. Then rush him to the doctor for further treatment. Be sure to take the bottle which contained the drug along with you. This will save time as the doctor sees just what drug has been taken and how much. He can then proceed with proper treatment.

One mother keeps a chart of common poisons with their antidotes tacked inside her kitchen cupboard for quick access if needed. These charts are available from your hospital emergency center or physician.

## Food Poisoning

During the summertime, with frequent picnics on the agenda, comes another poison danger. Government nutrition experts warn that summer-warmed kitchens offer the proper climate for bacteria. Slicers, grinders, and cutting boards must be kept cleaner, quicker. With proper warmth and enough time some strains of staphylococcus breed disease and cause toxins, warns Dr. Karla Longree, Cornell University's nutrition research expert. No amount of heating will remove such toxin if carried into food.

Acidity discourages the growth of bacteria, so use plenty of vinegar, lemon juice, pickles and relishes in your salads and sandwiches. If you must travel several hours before eating, freeze the sandwiches beforehand. They'll be ready to eat by the time you arrive at your picnic site, or carry food in ice coolers. You'll want to have only pleasant memories from your picnic!

## Dangerous Times of the Day

According to Dr. Ruth Lawrence of the University of Rochester's Poison Control Center, the most dangerous times of the day for child poisonings are breakfast and lunch. It's not what the kiddies eat, but what they get into while mother is busy preparing the meals. Most of the victims are under five years of age—more boys than girls.

"How can I keep my eyes on the children at the same time I prepare their meals?" you question. Even the three-year-old can help you with simple meal preparation, or sit on the counter and watch, or help set the table. Let Jacky or Dot carry unbreakable items to the table. Keep special coloring books or building blocks on hand to pull out only at these times while they sit in a corner near you. Perhaps an older

child can read favorite stories and help entertain the younger
ones.

## BURNS

In addition to possible poisoning and skin irritations,
burns are a very frequent hazard, for children may touch hot
objects.

In the event of such an accident, run cold tap water over
the burn, or soak it in cold water, or in any other cold, clean
harmless neutral fluid (such as milk—but not alcohol or fruit
juices). Switch to clean water as soon as possible if you use a
substitute in an emergency.

Under the tap, take care that the water pressure doesn't
break or injure the skin. Don't apply dressings. Avoid break-
ing blisters. Keep the burned area in the water until the pain
has ceased.

"Cold water is an effective first-aid device for burns and
scalds, and a pain-killer as well," says Dr. O. J. Ofeigsson of
Iceland.

On burns that cannot be submerged, apply ice wrapped in
cloth or a clean cloth soaked in ice water and change frequently until pain is gone.

A British physician recommends another cure for burns:
cold milk. Dr. Willington made his discovery quite by
chance when a woman patient accidentally scalded herself
severely. She plunged her hand in the nearest cold fluid—a
pitcher of milk. She kept it in for about a half hour.

The doctor then tried this simple remedy on more than
two-hundred burn victims. It proved effective for both first-
and second-degree burns. But it had to be applied immediately and compresses of cold milk kept over the burn for
the first twenty-four hours. Milk is handy in the kitchen
where most burns occur.

I personally know this to be true. One day I severely burned my finger with hot grease. I kept it in cold milk for some time. Then I loosely wrapped the finger with a cold milk-soaked cloth, tied a plastic bag around the hand, leaving it for several hours. Later in the day I removed the cloth. Although the burn was severe, it healed nicely without a blister.

## CAREFUL PARENTS

Well, as long as children are alive, I'm sure there will be accidents. We can trust God's protecting hand upon our homes. But this isn't a ticket for us to be careless and unconcerned. No! As parents we will enforce safety rules. We'll remove that which may cause accidents. We'll go out of our way to change shelves, change some personal likes or dislikes, or put on locks if necessary.

We'll use all precautions, and according to the researchers, our best caution is for us to keep healthy, keep close tab on the youngest child, and train children to keep away from possible dangers. Then trust them to their guardian angels!

## EMOTIONAL AND SPIRITUAL SAFETY

Physical safety in the home is important, but more important is emotional and spiritual safety. Just as you take precautions against physical harm, similarly you need to take measures to guard your child from evil, vice, crime, and moral poisons surrounding him on every side.

Are you aware of your actions and attitudes that may prove disastrous to your child's mental health? Are you content, happy, understanding, loving? Or do caustic words, complaining, loud speaking, or anger leave lifetime marks on his character?

Have you removed trashy literature and books, foul language, greed, self-centeredness as hindrances to his emotional and spiritual safety? Have you placed in your home good books, wholesome entertainment and recreation, inspiring music? Have you planned for family fun, fellowship, and companionship? Have you given God and His Word first place in your heart and home?

All these plus a vital faith in Jesus Christ, must be ingredients used in making your house a home which insures emotional and spiritual safety for your child. He can then go out from home and safely meet life in a hostile world.

# 11

# The Family Cooperates

There are several key words to successful living, one of which is cooperation.

We know what it means in the factory, on the highway, in business, in the classroom, in the hospital. It's talked about and experienced daily in these areas.

According to the dictionary, cooperation implies to help each other, work with, assist, support, relieve, encourage each other, "to act with one another." I like these words, don't you?

It's doing things together. It's taking time to share one's thoughts and ideas and dreams with each other. It's having fun times together and work, too.

It's closely related to interdependence—a depending on each other. Perhaps more important is meeting the other person's needs—not so much expecting him/her to meet your needs and desires.

## WHERE COOPERATION BEGINS

What comes to your mind when you hear the word *cooperation?* Do you think of family cooperation?

We don't hear much about cooperation in the home, on the

family level—yet I have a feeling that's where it all begins. Sounds good to me!

With whom does cooperation begin? . . . With the teen-ager? Who sets the example? . . . The kids? Not really. Cooperation begins with the husband and wife as they assume the tasks and privileges of marriage.

Bob comes home, tired out from the hassle all day at the office. A cooperative wife notes his feelings. She doesn't immediately barrage him with a list of chores he should do—or make negative remarks. She'll offer him a refreshing drink. See that he's comfortable. Perhaps she'll just be cheerful—with the house in order and a tempting meal cooking on the stove. If he prefers—a tussle with the kids to relax him.

A cooperative husband also senses his wife's feelings and needs. He relates to her in a helpful, encouraging, positive way.

## PAUL'S EXPERIENCE

Paul relates what a sense of cooperation—to work with each other—meant to him. Some months ago he began to feel a growing-apart in their marriage—in a number of little things. For one thing, his wife wasn't getting up to prepare breakfast like she used to do. Not that he ever asked her to, but she had wanted to because it pleased him. He decided to tell her about her neglect but wanted time to think it over.

Then one day at work he began talking to the Lord about it. Well, the Lord had a different approach. The Lord told him to start helping her in the evening. He started to argue, "*Me* help her? I work hard all day in the lumber camp with hardly a minute of rest. She's got it made—at home all day!" The Lord kept talking. That evening after a hot, tired day he came home, greeted her cheerfully, then inquired, "Honey, is there anything I can help you with?"

He meant it. In total sincerity his love came through. He helped with supper and with the children. It was a beautiful evening. The following morning his wife got up and prepared his breakfast. She *wanted* to!

That's cooperation—for this couple—in the way it suited them.

## LOVE IS THE ROOT

Love is the root of cooperation. This motivates interaction. It's only natural for each to have those areas in which he or she assumes responsibility. But it's unfortunate when husband and wife have stereotyped ideas of the other one's role—and there dare be no crossing over the boundaries.

John sits snugly in his easy chair with the paper and scolds Betty because the meal isn't on time and the children are too noisy. He could cooperate and entertain the children, or help out with the meal preparation.

Betty sees him struggling with his accounts but decides that she's entitled to a few moments for herself. She continues reading the novel.

Love sees the occasion to act together—then seizes the opportunity to do so!

Diane is seriously thinking about husband-wife relationships as she contemplates her future marriage. She believes cooperation is basic to good marital relationships. "Cooperation between husband and wife is so essential to joy and contentment." The self-centered husband or wife is unhappy and dissatisfied. In spite of all unselfish aims, no one is perfect. Sometimes we fail or forget. Thank God we don't need to stay down. By His help we forgive each other, and forget the past, then start over again.

## Parental Cooperation

I've purposely focused on husband and wife acting together—cooperating—as this is basic to family cooperation. The child and young person who's able "to act with another," as the dictionary defines cooperation, has learned it at home. How to cooperate is caught, not taught—caught from observing mother and father cooperating in the daily situations. The child cooperates because he's learned how from his parents. Infants and young children are natural imitators. They do what they see others do, although they don't know what the behavior means.

Dr. Leland Glover, well-known psychologist, marriage counselor, and educator, says that parents who want their child to behave in a certain way need to "cultivate that pattern of behavior" themselves. If you want the child to be cooperative, you will need to be cooperative. In *How to Give Your Child a Good Start in Life* Dr. Glover emphasizes, "By your deeds, not your words, will your child know you; by your deeds, not your words, he will learn."

## Needs Guidance

When the child's at the age he begins to interact, he needs guidance and direction, all the while observing.

The toddler enjoys doing things for you, as parents. You're proud that he brings his shoes to you to put on his feet. Or places them in the closet where they belong when he takes them off. He picks up toys nicely.

But what about the evening when you want to tidy up the room. His daddy's coming home any minute. Then it 'll be supper, fun time, and his bedtime. You ask Teddy, age two, to "please pick up the toys." He doesn't hear and continues to play. Nor does he respond the second time you mention it.

Then's the time to suggest by saying, "Let's pick up your

toys. I'll help you." If you do this in love, he'll sense your feeling and want to help you. You can laugh with him and talk about Daddy coming home soon, as together you put the toys away.

If, on the other hand, you lecture about those being his toys, not yours, and how ugly the floor looks, he'll be less apt to pick them up. He isn't able to understand the meaning of personal property.

Getting irritated at him for not picking up the toys isn't teaching cooperation—but doing it together in a happy mood is.

At a later age he may need some form of discipline—to help him learn to obey and take responsibility. At an early age children *want* to cooperate. They enjoy doing things with Mom and Dad. Very early they catch the meaning of cooperation. This is good. It's important to life.

Family cooperation: when family members are able to act with each other, to do things together in a happy, helpful way.

## CHILDREN DEFINE COOPERATION

What do children think about cooperation?

If I were to ask your son or daughter, "What is family cooperation?" would the answer be as one child's response was, "When everyone works together"?

That's a good answer.

Albert says that he is learning to cooperate. "My sister and I take turns doing the dishes every day. We have to clean our rooms and do our homework before we watch TV every day when we get home from school."

Bobby says, "I got a dog and my sister's got a cat. My brother's got fish. We have to feed the fish every other day. We don't always feed them, but if we don't we get in trouble."

When asked if he thinks it's good to have chores Bobby replied, "It's good to have chores. Because then you learn responsibility."

When asked if it's important to work with their father and mother Johnny responded: "Yeah, 'cause you learn how to do it better by watching them. Like if you see your dad fixing the roof or something, you could do it a lot better after you watched him when you're a little older than if you hadn't watched him."

Betty commented: ". . . Every spring when my grandmother and I plant the garden she's always telling me tips on how to make your rows grow better and what to do with your soil and how to make your plants grow larger."

It's great to see parents and children, grandparents, too, cooperating in the job that has to be done. This, however, seems to be absent in many homes.

## RESPONSIBILITY FOR CHORES

It's well for parents to assign a responsibility to each child. In those early years, you show him how, helping him to do the task. In later years, he makes it his own responsibility.

Often parents chart the child's daily chores. Each day he/she checks them off. They may encourage the child getting the chores done by allowing him to do something he likes after the assignment is completed.

This is all good. It's one form of cooperation in getting the work done that's required of family living—each doing his own chores.

## COOPERATE TOGETHER

There's also another way to cooperate, as the children mentioned: It's doing things together.

This is beautiful to observe—mother and children together

preparing the meal, the table, and cleaning up afterwards, doing the laundry weekly, cleaning, or baking. Dad and sons cooperating in yard and farm work, in building something. All the family together: clearing the basement, raking leaves, doing yard work or farm chores.

This is very important to family living. Perhaps more important than each doing his or her own specific chores. Yet, I'm amazed at the number of moms and dads who don't allow their children this learning experience—of doing things together.

One child remarked, "I don't do any work. My mom doesn't like us to wash dishes. She says we waste too much soap."

I know a mother who denied her children the privilege of cooperating with her because, "They make such a mess."

Another mother complains, "They're in my way. I can do it quicker by myself!" Dads say the same thing.

It seems to me these parents are getting their values mixed up. Teaching the child cooperation should take priority over having to buy more soap, or clean up a mess, or take a few extra more minutes to do the job, don't you think?

## COOPERATION—KEY WORD

Cooperation is important in *all* areas of family living. It may occasionally mean caring for the one who may be ill, even doing his job for him.

Cooperating should carry over in fun times, in worship experiences, in helping with lessons and projects.

That's why God made families—for children to learn how to live harmoniously and happily together with adults through cooperation and caring. To learn true values of life. To learn about God and His truths.

*Cooperation*—a key word to successful family living!

# 12

# The House for You

I'd like to peek inside your house—and observe how you have made your house into a home.

I'm reminded now of Sally who lives in a city-housing development. The exterior resembles all the other units. But open the door and it is *different!* Oh yes, the rooms are painted according to regulations. However, they reflect *her*—her personality.

Sally has gotten much of her furnishings here and there. Some given to her. Yet the moment you open the door you see her warmth and taste and individuality expressed in the pictures, the doilies, the plants, the throw rugs, and other little touches. Sally keeps her home clean and in order—as much as possible with three little ones at home.

She could complain about what she can't do, about what she doesn't have. Instead she adds her personal touch. She puts her heart and love into what she has. She has made a home out of a house—a trait common to us women.

## "BORN NESTERS"

"Female creatures are born nesters. Give them anything walled and covered over from the weather—a cabin, a tent, a

115

trailer, even a dormitory room . . . most of them will manage to turn it into a home. They will decorate the walls, invent a rug or a table, plant something green in a pot, and settle there snug as mice in their burrows.'' So states Phyllis McGinley in her popular book, *Sixpence in Her Shoe*.

A young girl recently moved into our community. She spent many hours apartment-hunting and was delighted when she located one unfurnished—in need of repairs, paint, and general fix-up. She spent many hours planning and decorating the rooms. She improvised furniture. She's experienced a delightful satisfaction turning the few rooms into a home—soon to be complete with a husband.

We women seem to be able to take a look at what we have at hand and utilize it!

## EVERYONE NEEDS A HOUSE

Everyone needs a house into which we put our home. It's natural to desire our personal roof—a place to call our own.

Unfortunately, in many areas of the world women don't have this privilege. We need to thank God for this blessing we've taken for granted.

Did you choose your house? or did you set up housekeeping in what was available—like many young homemakers have to do? It may be a room or two in the parental house; or the apartment the husband lived in; or the only one available close to his job or school. Perhaps a mobile home.

Some couples are able to rent a house. Still others buy or build their own. In the latter case, the homemaker helps make decisions as to the type of house.

The amount of money available (whether loan or savings or inheritance) usually says a lot about the house one rents, builds, or buys. Jobs, how many children (or none) also influence one's choice.

Every spring hundreds of couples get the urge to go house-hunting. They may be young couples with a child or two who've outgrown their small apartment; also those who've gotten a raise or transferred to a new job; perhaps it's the older couples whose house has outgrown them.

## RIGHT FOR YOU

Everyone wants the Perfect House, don't they? Perhaps that's not to be found.

We've lived in eleven different houses since our marriage. I've visited in hundreds—and I have yet to see one that's *perfect*. Even those who build sometimes end up with too big or too little closets, perhaps placed wrongly, or with congested areas.

Upon our return from the mission field, there were two places available—a house in the country and an apartment close to the college where my husband taught. We chose the house in the country, although it was very small. The children had free range of the yard and countryside, in contrast to the apartment in a populated area.

After several years of renting, we bought a house close to the school. My husband could walk to his classes. The acreage included a large yard, garden plot, and chicken houses for raising broilers. These would provide jobs for our four growing children. The house was not my "dream house," but it met our family needs at that time.

Since we now are only two and not as able to care for the yard and garden, we have thoughts of house-hunting again.

## CONSIDER POSSIBILITIES

If you consider moving, you need to question, "What are some advantages and disadvantages of the different areas?" The country has it's advantages—nature's beauty, less congested. It has its problems. You need to cope with transportation, both summer and winter—and cope with aloneness, with distance from the stores.

The city offers the widest range of rentals. Less money goes into transportation, but there are more attractions to spend money—proximity of stores, theaters, concerts, and museums.

The suburb seems ideal for many families. Here are greater opportunities for community and social life. But then there are dangers of wanting to become like everyone else!

If you're house-hunting, and have decided on the area, you'll want to let all your acquaintances know about it. They may be able to give you some clues. Watch the ads in the newspaper. Walk, or drive up and down the streets and roads.

If you rent, clear with the landlord concerning his specifications. Read the lease carefully before signing. Have on paper an agreement about maintenance and care.

## A Way of Life

Mary Davis Gillies, Decorating and Building Editor of *McCall's,* says the couple who buys or decides to build, is establishing a way of life for the family; is also giving future time to care and repair of a house. It's a major investment. She feels it's important "to know yourself." Know who you are—whether working with a $3,500 or a $35,000 budget. Know your aims, goals, and ambitions for your family. And don't get sidetracked by "what others are doing." Be realistic.

Mrs. Gillies has suggested you can afford a house double your income. (Perhaps that's not a sure guide now with prices skyrocketing!)

Your house is not for anyone else—not for your sister or

friend or advisers. It's the one for you. You accept it on this basis. You realize that you need to focus on the advantages, on what's right about it, rather than on the disadvantages —whether you prefer an exotic house, with glass walls, or one with half a dozen or more gables and extensions, a simple *A*-frame house, the ranch-style, a mobile home, or the sturdy, old, abandoned house that's stood the years. *Whichever*—you'll know the one for you! You know what you can afford, where you need to live, and what meets the needs of your family. In such a major decision, you'll want to let God help you find the place—just for you!

## You Buy

If you have chosen to buy a house, you may want to decorate and furnish it. Again, consider necessary fundamentals of your goal, your life-style, the atmosphere you enjoy—simple, festive, luxurious, cultural, colonial, or French.

You need to know with what you feel comfortable. What makes your family members comfortable at this stage of their lives. Perhaps this calls for temporarily changing the use of some rooms. You may turn the dining room into a nursery, or the big hall into another bedroom. If you have teen-agers, you may enclose the porch and make it into a recreation room. You'll furnish the rooms according to the goals you have in mind for the family's usage. Decorating and furnishing a house should focus on comfort and convenience, not merely appearance.

If you plan on redecorating the entire house, begin upstairs. Complete it before you tackle the first floor to eliminate workers tracking through the house. It also makes it possible for you to clean after them room by room.

## Decorating Hints

Daryl V. Hoole, in her book, *The Art of Homemaking,* gives some basic decorating hints. The well-decorated room "serves its purpose and is pleasing in appearance, not just that it follows certain rigid rules. Rooms should be able to be lived in and should also be a source of pride to the residents . . . Each item in the house should fulfill its function."

Daryl advises "unification of a theme." You want "a good transition of color from one room to the next; furniture and accessories should be compatible in style. The accessories should lend enrichment . . . Each room should have a comfortable feeling of balance."

Color is important. It's good to "have one predominating color in a room." Choose colors of furniture and accessories which blend.

She suggests you can easily remember this formula: "Something dark and something light. Something dull and something bright."

You'll want to know the type of merchandise available. Read newspaper ads. Look in various stores before buying.

## You Build

If you are one of the fortunate families planning to build, you may wish to plot a plan of each room—indicate the location of doors, windows, stairways, and where you want your furniture, play area, storage space, laundry and other special areas.

A friend of mine drew that kind of floor plan for her house. She made movable objects for each piece of furniture, moving them according to what seemed best for her family. She lived with her plan for several months, and tried to think of all advantages or disadvantages in the plan. She changed it frequently, settling on the one best suited for her family.

## You Improvise

Perhaps you're one of those couples that has had to start out on a shoestring. You've had to improvise furniture for the time being. I'll share with you what others have done.

One couple bought a sofa at an auction, refinished the wood, and covered the cushions with sturdy denim and a contrast-color edging. It was very attractive.

You can make a TV stand out of two sturdy suitcases. Stand them on end, make a square top and sew a four-sided valance. Make a coffee table from an old door. Cut it the size you want and glue the end strip back on. Place it on either wooden or wrought-iron legs and paint it; or use an old treadle sewing machine for the stand.

Colored or figured sheets can be used for drapes. Make bookshelves from inexpensive boards. Support these shelves with bricks. You may wish to paint or varnish the boards or cover them. That's what our daughter-in-law did. She covered the boards with an inexpensive burlap-type material and sprayed the bricks a contrasting color. It looks very attractive.

Diane's round table is an electric-wire wooden spool setting on end, covered with a cloth. Her chairs (temporarily) are kegs from a country store, which she has painted.

## Kind of Living

I've been talking about the house for you. The kind of house we live in is important, to be sure, but what really counts is the kind of living that goes on in the house!

I've been in homes—I'm sure you have too—that were cluttered. I'm thinking of one that needed painting. The furniture and furnishings represented various themes; toys scattered on the floor; bits of material lying near the sewing machine. But I felt warmth and a welcome. After one initial glance, I forgot the appearance.

What happened? The homemaker didn't need to apologize. She was secure in her way of life. Happy family living was more important than a meticulous house.

Don't misunderstand me: I'm not advising dirty floors, walls, table, and counters! Neither filthy corners, unmade beds and smelly, dirty clothes and dishes. I believe meeting the family's interests and needs, keeping them occupied and happy, supersedes having everything in its place.

I also recall another home I once visited—ranch-style, matching, luxurious furniture, correct decor, furnishings, and decoration. Every room like a page in a house magazine. The children came into the room gingerly, to sit in a perfect posture. There was no response from the parents. I felt terribly uncomfortable in a sterile atmosphere. The cold feeling impressed me more than did the perfect house.

## ATMOSPHERE

Flowers and plants add a touch of beauty to your home —both indoors and outdoors (if this is possible). Tantalizing odors from freshly baked rolls, cakes, pies, bread, or from a roast or chili con carne—all these help make your home's atmosphere. They create hominess and attraction. Help make it a place where each family member feels relaxed and comfortable, wants to come home to—and friends enjoy returning to.

Take pride in your house. Be interested in it. Make it into a home which reflects you, and your family's personality. Use your creativity and imagination.

It should be a place where God is the "unseen guest at

every meal, the silent listener to every conversation" and where His ideas are obeyed and enjoyed.

## THAT PERFECT HOME

I believe every woman has her dream home. We appreciate certain features. We dislike others. I have a definite list of what I like and don't like. I've saved various house plans; have drawn some of my own, then changed these.

Long ago I realized that I may never find my dream house on this earth. Besides, it's temporary. A house basically is a shelter—place of protection, privacy, rest, and nourishment—physical, emotional and spiritual. However, I'm looking forward to that perfect house (and home) in heaven. Until then, I want to make the house I live in a home where there's an atmosphere of love, warmth, kindness, hospitality, joy, peace, and Presence of my Lord.

# 13

# You Move Again

Your husband unexpectedly announces, "Guess what—the company wants to transfer me to Farland."

You probably gasp and exclaim, "What? We just moved here three years ago. The children and I have become a part of this community. We feel at home."

Husband calmly answers, "It's a raise, you know."

## ON THE MOVE

As difficult as it is to be uprooted from one's home and community and friends, we are a mobile society. About 20 percent of the American population moves yearly.

Moving is difficult. It's lots of hard work. For some it's a traumatic experience.

It *can* be a challenging experience, an adventure of faith and courage as you carefully plan, prepare, and pray about the move.

You'll consider what the move means to your husband. You'll also want to discuss the idea with the family. The approach you take will depend on their ages.

## A FAMILY DECISION

Susan says they told the family (two teen-agers and a nine-year-old) about her husband's offer to teach at a college several hundred miles distant. They discussed all the factors involved. They listened to each other. They prayed together. It was an open issue. As things happened the children could say, "Hey, Mom, what about this if we move?" But ultimately the decision was Daddy's to make.

One very beautiful afternoon the father and nine-year-old son were taking a walk and the son said, "I don't want to leave my friends. I don't want to move, but I want to do what God wants us to do. Promise me, Daddy, you won't listen to the preacher, or any other man, but just to God."

They moved several months ago. They've had some difficult adjustments but are on top now. The family cooperating in the decision—subject to God's will for them —contributed to making these adjustments effectively.

After the decision was made to move, the family visited their new location—the schools, the shopping center, the churches. They discussed what these had to offer and compared them with the schools and churches they were used to.

## MAKE PLANS

Like Susan and her family, you've arrived at your decision. You're moving.

Now you begin planning. You'll draw on your past experiences, remembering the boo-boos and the lessons learned from previous moves. You'll talk to your neighbor, Betty, who's moved five times.

How will you move? This is essential. You'll need to mentally take inventory of your furniture, clothing, household possessions, and decide what you should take along, or discard, or sell, or give to a charitable institution.

It'll help to make a checklist of duties, and a schedule to follow as you begin packing.

If you move by yourself (hiring a rental-trailer or truck) you can take only part of your possessions, or—you may have a sale and move only your personal belongings.

## THE MOVERS COME

If a moving company moves you, contact them early for instructions. Many provide helpful booklets on "How to Move." Some give you the option to do the packing, and they do the loading. Other companies choose to do both the packing and unpacking. Either way, you'll need to pack some personal belongings and the perishables.

Plan to be there when the movers come. They appreciate you telling them, "I want those items in this room packed. These items we'll take." On the other hand, they don't want someone standing over their shoulder telling how to do everything. What they want is for you to be available, to answer the questions that might arise.

Number the pieces of furniture and give the movers a floor plan of your new home. They'll correctly place the furniture, if you're not there when the furniture arrives.

## START TO PACK EARLY

It takes time to get everything packed. You'll need to start early. Nancy says she started six weeks ahead of their moving—beginning with items she wouldn't need during that period. She labeled each box (its contents and where it was to go: ATTIC, MASTER BEDROOM, KITCHEN, and so forth. When her in-laws helped unpack the trailer they knew just where to put the things. She also identified where to place the few pieces of furniture they moved.

Mary suggests packing food in a basket for your first meal to take with you in the car. Throw in a towel, soap, and washcloth, too. In another basket (or bag), pack the night clothes for the family, including toothpaste, combs, and all the personal items you'll need for the first night.

## UTILITIES

Before you abandon your house, you need to make arrangements with proper persons when to cut off gas, electricity, water, and phone.

In the place where you're going you'll need to contact the companies as soon as possible to have them hook up these utilities. The Chamber of Commerce is glad to give you the proper information, or municipal officials. And don't forget to arrange to have your mail forwarded through the post office. By giving magazines and other periodicals your new address at least six weeks ahead of your move you will save expensive forwarding fees.

## PRIORITIES

You have moved. Now you're probably looking around at the drapeless windows, the boxes and cluttered-up rooms and asking, "What shall I do first? Where do I begin?"

It looks sort of hopeless, doesn't it? Do remember that you won't get everything in order the first day, or the next. But you will eventually.

Start with getting the beds made. And have a few kitchen items and food in place so you can prepare breakfast the next morning.

Put some of your prettiest sheets at the big windows. Tack towels at the small ones until you can get what you want and need.

The most important thing is to be sensitive to the family's needs. This is top priority.

## FAMILY NEEDS

Susan said after their move when she stood in the middle of chaos, she prayed, "Lord, help me know what is most important for the family now. In the light of eternity this mess doesn't really matter."

This approach gave her the right frame of mind to be sensitive to her husband's, to the children's, and her own emotional and spiritual needs, as well as the immediate physical needs.

She sensed some of the children wanted to be with her all the time, offering to do jobs for her. They were lonely, so she spent more time with them.

For the younger children the first day will be full of excitement. It's fun to help unpack and place things properly. They'll also come to show you what they've discovered outside. (They may even bring in a new friend!) Regardless of age, the child will need extra attention,

## ACQUAINT YOURSELF WITH COMMUNITY

As soon as possible, acquaint the children with the location of the school, if you didn't make a visit prior to moving. Tour the community recreational facilities and shopping area. Ask someone you have confidence in about doctors and dentists.

If your move is into a Welcome Wagon area, you're fortunate, because already the hostess has visited you and informed you of the locations of those services you need —stores, bank, laundromat, cleaners, and so on.

Maybe your moving has been made easier because a

neighbor welcomed you—brought in your first meal, or invited you over to eat with them.

The church-going family has an advantage. They easily become familiar with the new community through the church family. Very frequently they have a welcoming group or individual who makes you feel at home immediately. They may provide some meals those first days, and be available to assist you in finding what you need.

Mary says the single woman often has difficulty getting acquainted. There are no children to quickly find friends. No husband who immediately relates to co-workers. She herself needs to put forth a greater effort to take the initiative to strike up a conversation when she meets another occupant of the same apartment on the elevator, or near the building. She can ask the location of the bank, or when the garbage is collected, making this a point of contact and fellowship.

A sense of humor helps in your adjusting to new surroundings, in adapting to changes.

## The Forward Look

It helps, too, to have the "forward look," which our local Welcome Wagon Hostess emphasizes. Instead of focusing on the past and comparing everything with the way it used to be, take a forward look at your goals. Take a positive look at who you and your family are, look at where you are, at the neighborhood, the privileges and opportunities God presents you each day.

A move into a new job, new house, and community can be a blessing and challenge.

Susan says she and her family rested in the confidence that God led them in their move. He was with them. This confidence carried them through many new, perhaps frightening, adjustments. God can do the same for you.

# 14

# The Gift of Hospitality

How long has it been since you've invited someone to eat with you and your family?

Do you enjoy entertaining?

Are you known for your hospitality?

Many homemakers hesitate to entertain because they feel they don't have the essentials. They make excuses: "If only I had a larger dining room . . . or I'll wait until I get my new china . . . or until the room's painted . . . I have such an old stove . . . my fondue set is outdated."

To be sure, many of us don't have everything we'd like to have. But we shouldn't allow our lacks to keep us from inviting our friends over occasionally, or entertaining overnight guests.

I admire one young couple. The husband wrote to his grandmother telling of a meal a group of them enjoyed in another young couple's home. He mentioned, "They're another couple that live on the floor like we do. They didn't have enough chairs to go around!"

## WELCOME—FROM THE HEART

After all, the physical comforts are not the main factor in hospitality—not what the guest remembers. He enjoys a comfortable bed—is grateful for tasty food. But mostly he recalls the friendliness, the acceptance as part of the family—around the table in conversation, and in the routine details. The welcome: This comes from your heart, not your head.

Perhaps you've got a tight schedule, and think you can't entertain. You can be hospitable—if you remember this important rule: Relax, take it easy.

If you think you need heaps of fancy food, or shiny windows and floors, or the latest in china, then you won't entertain—or be completely worn out if you do!

It's up to each of us to do what we can.

"Hospitality is one of the cardinal virtues," says the famous author and housewife, Phyllis McGinley.

We dare not let this slip away from us! Some people believe it's already gone.

## Unexpected Guests

It's challenging to open your heart and home to overnight guests—especially the unexpected ones. Welcome them —friends or strangers—but not grudgingly, not merely because you feel obligated. This doesn't count. Hospitality is a gift everyone appreciates. Hospitality cannot be grudgingly a duty.

The secret in such unexpected situations is to offer what you have: a cot, or daybed (even though it's a three-quarter bed). One of the children's rooms will be sufficient. It should be reasonably clean, aired out, clean sheets, blankets, with an extra blanket handy. Ever since I, as a guest myself, shivered through a night with my coat thrown on the bed, and the extra pillow over my feet, I have consciously tried to supply sufficient bedding.

When you show your guest to the room, also show the

necessary light switches, both in the room and the hall. Point out the location of the bathroom and the guest towels. Provide extra closet space and hangers.

## SHARE PLANS

Depending on your guest's interests, provide writing space on a table or desk, perhaps some interesting books. If your guest stays for any length of time, provide a clean dresser drawer. Place straight pins and a few safety pins in a tray, and a box of tissues. One hostess leaves a new tooth brush still in the plastic container on the dresser.

Before retiring, discuss plans for the breakfast hour and the following day. Remember to keep uppermost in mind the guest's comfort and interests. Allow the guest the privilege to plan and to choose what appeals to him/her for the few hours you can spend together.

## ENJOY GUESTS

Although I'm not able to entertain as frequently as I'd like to, I do enjoy having guests in our home. As a family we're grateful for the hearts and homes that have been opened to us—in many states and in other countries.

Much of my entertaining is having friends and relatives from far away who are passing through to stop off at our house, rather than inviting neighbors and friends living in my community. Someday, hopefully, I'll have time to be more hospitable to those living nearby.

On-the-spot entertaining also comes about since we live close to private boarding schools which our children attended. They'd bring friends home very frequently.

Our son, Martin, brought us the most guests. He enjoyed tinkering with motors. Frequently a classmate living in the dormitory would be helping him—both completely oblivious to the time. His friend would miss his meal at the dining hall. Martin would call into the house (about five minutes before supper) and say, "Mom, he's going to stay for supper, okay? He doesn't eat much!" During the winter months when a buddy of his couldn't get home—snowbound—we'd fix up an extra plate, extra bed, or sleeping bag.

## Becomes Easier

Would you believe it? This'd happen most often when I'd get home late and would quickly stir up a meal. But, we always had enough. And invariably my home-baked bread saved the day. I have yet to see the boy who can't fill up on home-baked bread, butter and honey or jam, when necessary! Home-canned fruit is also readily accepted and enjoyed. I've learned to keep in stock canned meat, and quickly prepared meat dishes.

It hasn't always been easy for me to accept my husband's announcement, "I've invited so-and-so to lunch—to dinner—to stay here during the convention." But the more I do it, the easier it becomes.

## An Attitude of Welcome

Remember, hospitality is an attitude of welcome—toward friends, neighbors, visiting persons, or families in the community. Share your home. Share yourself—your family. Invite a family over for an evening of food and fun, or just couples after children are asleep. Serve nutritious but simple foods. And be sure to have plenty.

Enlist each member to help you prepare and serve the meal—whether indoors or outdoors—and with the cleaning up afterwards. They'll enjoy the time of fun and fellowship together if you do.

## CHILDREN AND GUESTS

Guests enjoy children. Introduce them properly and teach them how to greet newcomers—how to offer suggestions such as: "May I take your coat?" "Please be seated," or, "Would you like a cold drink?" (If it's winter offer a hot drink!)

I recall one hot summer day when we arrived at my brother's home. And almost immediately their eight-year-old daughter, Marla, suggested, "Would you like a drink of lemonade?" You already know our answer! She then proceeded to the kitchen and in no time at all appeared with big glasses of refreshing lemonade. Mind you, all this without any coaching or help from her mother!

## THE LONERS AND STRANGERS

There are many lonely persons, especially those who move in from other communities. One out of five moves every year. And I know how lonesome one can get during those first days and weeks. To be welcomed and invited into a home can completely change attitudes about the people, the community.

There are other lonely people nearby—the singles, the widows, the aged couple. They enjoy fellowship with others around a delicious meal. Imagine how often (how infrequently) they prepare a dinner of meat, potatoes, gravy, vegetables, salad, and dessert!

Not only should your home be open to friends, relatives, and neighbors, but also to the stranger. "Never refuse to extend your hospitality to strangers" is a command from the Good Book. In fact, God insinuates that by so doing you may be entertaining an angel, even God Himself. (*See* Hebrews 13:2.)

If there's an orphanage in the community, open your home to a child for several weeks, or contact an agency instrumental in helping inner-city children find homes for two or three weeks during the summer months.

## MINISTERING TO OTHERS

Author Mary La Grand Bouma states in *The Creative Homemaker,* "The happiest and most fulfilled homemakers are those who are consistently ministering to others in addition to their own families."

Very recently I was a guest in the home of a happy homemaker who has experienced this truth. I felt loved and welcomed from the moment I arrived until the moment I left. The younger son shared his room. The teen-ager missed morning classes to drive his mother to the airport to meet me. The father and son did the supper dishes so we could make our appointments.

The hostess and her family have had a complete change of life—their goals, attitudes, life-style—since they've allowed Jesus Christ to control their daily living—and not they, themselves.

During my stay, I discovered that Ann now has as her goal making a happy home for her husband and children. She willingly gave up some of her own personal interests in order to make this possible. Her family is thrilled, and appreciative, and have found this same love and joy in Christ.

She also has opened her home to others. Every week women gather together in her home from every type of life—the wealthy and the not-so-wealthy; the educated and not-so-educated—those of various colors and faiths, or with no faith.

Ann personally relates to many others. Her home is open to couples with problems. They all feel welcome. The hospitality, the warmth, the sincerity envelop everyone. They return. In returning they find healing and hope, and new life through Ann's secret—relating to Jesus Christ.

## A Gift of Love

In our selfish, self-centered, thing-oriented culture, people have almost forgotten how to open their hearts and homes to others. That's why it's so refreshing to find the Anns and their families still existing in today's society.

Entertaining is fun. It's rewarding as you form new acquaintances, learn about other countries, other projects, other cultures.

Entertaining is inspiring, making you forgetful of the extra work as you share together—as you share your faith and love for Jesus Christ.

Hospitality is love. Then things, or lack of them, move into proper focus. The idea of perfection vanishes. In their places appear the rewards. Pleasant memories of such occasions mean much to you.

Hospitality is a gift of love—a gift to be shared with others.

# 15

# Get Rid of the Blahs

What do you do when you have the blahs? What causes them?

It could be: lack of motivation, lack of desire to enjoy this homemaking career, perhaps no goals in mind. Some women feel unappreciated. Some believe they are "wasting their training, energy, and time on menial housekeeping chores." Others have given up a professional job (which they have enjoyed and were successful in). They miss the excitement and interaction with many persons.

Mary writes: "I was a librarian for six years. There are some days when I'd give anything to be back in the library instead of being at home. Have you anything to suggest?"

Edith comments, "I enjoy being with my family—but I miss the glamour and the people of my previous nursing career."

## OTHER CAUSES

Dot doesn't know how to be a homemaker. "I recently gave up my business to be the kind of mother I want to be. Because of neglect our son had gotten into serious trouble. But I'll be honest—as much as I want to be at home—I don't

139

know how to be a good mother and housekeeper. Can you help me?"

Jane wrote that she used to lie in bed until almost noon —not only on Monday but every morning! She'd let her husband get up, get his and the children's breakfasts, get them off to school, and himself to work. "I hated to get at the housework," she commented. "I was always tired! There was no catching up."

Jane's right. *There's no catching up.* As one woman stated, you go to bed at night with your work done, but while you sleep, "Sheets are wrinkling, dust is settling, and stomachs are getting empty."

Many homemakers, like Jane, detest the daily housekeeping chores. They're "bored to death." They also suffer from fatigue.

Some homemaker's boredom comes from being unprepared for their responsibilities. Their mothers never took time to teach them as Dorothy wrote: "When I wanted to help, mother would shoo me out of the kitchen saying, 'I can do it quicker myself.' It's been very difficult for me to do housekeeping. But I'm slowly learning."

Mrs. H. confesses she's bored. "I have too much leisure time and I end up doing nothing."

Mrs. M. was depressed "because I just couldn't keep up with my neighbor, Sally. Recently I honestly faced myself. I'm a slow person. Sally is hyper. I realize now I can't be her—I have to be myself."

Illness can cause fatigue—so can anxiety. But frequently homemaker's fatigue seems to be the result of constant daily stress. For this there is a remedy. According to Dr. Peter J. Steincrohm, "Thousands of men and women could relieve chronic fatigue by the simple process of planning ahead —and fighting procrastination."

If you have the blahs tell yourself they aren't necessary. Admitting them, and the causes for them, puts you on the right road to getting rid of them.

## MAXINE'S DISCOVERY

Maxine had to come to this place. She was a full-time homemaker but was bored, frustrated, hostile, desperate. In her desperation one night she cried out to God to help her. Suddenly a new power swept into her mind. She found herself counting her blessings—a home, a husband who still loved her, three healthy, happy children.

The thought occurred to her that God had given her children to love and care for, yet, she was daily screaming at them, hurting them. They were afraid of her. She was constantly nagging and complaining to her husband.

The next day Maxine asked God for love. Immediately she found herself giving love and kind words to the children, and fewer spankings.

She began to enjoy each moment. When the floor was cluttered she thanked God for healthy children.

She began to use the three magic words, "I love you." Her family responded joyfully to them!

## PEACE . . . JOY

Maxine now has goals beyond herself. They are to enjoy each moment, and to teach her children how to eat, how to drink, how to put things together, how to climb stairs, how to ride a bicycle. This basic learning can either be painful to both child and mother, or it can be a bond of love and patience between them.

"There are days when I'm tired, and have the blues," concludes Maxine, "but I keep counting my blessings and praying for guidance. The rewards have been many: the children's laughter, the many unexpected hugs and kisses, the happy look on my husband's face when he comes home at night, the fun of doing things as a family . . . and the peace of mind and inner joy I feel.'' (Maxine A. Braatz's story was reported in a *Scope* article, "I Came Back," and is used by permission.)

Peace of mind . . . inner joy . . . what a beautiful exchange for the blues and unhappiness!

### Trapped

Like Maxine, Barbara got rid of the blahs, but her experience was quite different.

She tells her story:

"I was just really dissatisfied with my role. I looked away from the situation that I was in. It just looked so good when the grass is greener on the other side of the fence. I am a nurse and when you are a nurse you really get the satisfaction of helping people. People appreciate you. I guess every housewife, at one time or other, just doesn't feel a bit appreciated. Basically that's a selfish attitude, it stems from within one's self and not really those that are around one.

"I hadn't always felt this way. I always enjoyed life and by nature I'm an outgoing person, but it was kind of a combination of things. I had had my third baby and he was a fussy baby. My husband was in school and also working a lot away from home. It seemed that I had to carry the load at home, and I got very resentful about it. One thing led to another thing that led to another thing, and just kept getting worse. Then the situation really got bad where I got so depressed I couldn't even half function at home. I was screaming at the children all of the time.''

## DISSATISFACTION WITH SELF

"My feeling of being trapped did not grow out of not being able to work; nor did it begin when I stopped nursing, because I stopped nursing when my first child was born and we moved to our present location several years later. And then to supplement my husband's income I went to work part-time and it was kind of an outlet for me. Kind of, you know, an easy way out. I enjoyed it and yet it really frustrated me because it made it much busier at home. There was so much more to cope with. I think basically, the problem with me was I didn't really want to be the kind of wife that I should be. Just a general dissatisfaction with myself.

"I had to start with my basic philosophy in life . . . starting out number one as being really a Jesus woman. You know, someone who really has a personal commitment to go the way of Jesus. I feel it's the kind of thing that can get me through the day."

## RENEWAL WITH GOD

"Then right along with that also is a basic philosophy about oneself. We have a tendency to feel like we don't compare with another woman. We're always comparing ourselves with someone else. I had to accept myself. That I'm a woman of God's design and exactly the way He wants me to be. As I began to appreciate the things about me that God has made for His honor and glory, then I began to be able to relate to someone else. I'm no longer working so hard, emotionally grappling with whether that person thinks I'm worth as much as another person.

"I overcame my feelings of frustration and defeat through a renewal experience with the Lord. I had gone to psychiatrists. During this time I had some friends and relatives who were quite concerned about my emotional as well as spiritual attitudes. They were spending a lot of time in prayer for us. I had an experience with the Lord that just completely changed my life. It's been just all that different ever since.''

## IN GIVING—YOU RECEIVE

''I now feel self-assured, happy, peaceful, and contented. Life just gets better all the time. It's the whole principle of giving and reaping. You know we talk about that when it comes to money but I think it really applies to life. The more that I give of myself, the more that I am concerned about being the kind of mother and wife that I need to be in my home, about giving up the right that I have to time, and so forth, the better mother I'll be. If I give of myself I'm going to receive and reap a lot more than I will by wanting to hold on to myself and having my own way.

''My change in attitude reflects in the family, and in my relationship with my husband. There's a big difference in the children. They are much happier. There still are times when something comes up that I really want to have it out and say my piece, but the Lord has taught me that that just isn't the way to do it, because you make yourself unhappy as well as those around you. I'm slowly learning to keep my mouth shut and to bite my tongue and to turn it over to the Lord, and it really works great.

''I say this for the sake of those who might feel that this is an unfair situation for a woman to be in, where she can't cope with her situation and wants to blame her husband. (And many times husbands are at fault, too.)''

## Outlets

"I also think while the woman gives up herself to her family, it's important that she also takes time out for herself. I read every book I get my hands on. If I have a book why I can really take a little vacation.

"One thing, too, that I got into during this blah depression time was soap operas and that is a no-no in my book now, because it was an escape from my own real world but not a very healthy escape. When it was over I still had to come back to what's real life. I got so involved in these stories that I didn't even want to have to do what I had to do at home. I have found other outlets which help me realistically face my household duties. I really enjoy people. I do a lot of visiting and have a lot of people in for lunch, ladies in during the week, and this type of thing.

"I love sports—a good outlet, too, if a person is sports-minded. I took tennis lessons about a year and a half ago and joined the local tennis league. That's a fantastic opportunity to meet people and to relate to people. It's good for me physically."

## Help Others

"It helps to get involved with other homemakers, especially one who's bored and frustrated. If you have this opportunity, stick with her closely. Let her know you're her friend. You care. Also that the Lord cares. Let His love flow through you to your family, and to others. The joy that comes from helping someone else overcome boredom makes my day!"

Maxine and Barbara hold no monopoly, no rights to the secret of joy and peace.

## GUIDELINES

Homemaker, you too can get rid of the blahs. Like these women, follow these steps:

1 *Admit how you feel,* about yourself as a woman, about your role and function as person, as wife, and mother.

2 *Accept yourself.*

3 *Share with a Christian confidant.*

4 *Pray and read the Word.*

5 *Renew your commitment to God.*

6 *Accept your situation*—your husband, family, house—as from God.

7 *Be a creative homemaker.*

8 *Find worthwhile outlets,* which you enjoy.

9 *Get interested in others* (begin with the family).

10 *Replace negative thoughts* with positive ones.

**God Is Love.** Draw from His unending, unlimited source. Let His love control your daily thoughts and actions.

# 16

# Why Bother?

You've washed about 135 thousand dishes in five years of married life. You've walked several miles daily (on the average), and spent a minimum of four hours daily doing housework. (That's twenty-eight hours weekly.) A grand total of 1,456 hours per year. *Minimum,* mind you! In ten years you've totaled 14,560 hours.

You've awakened several times during the night through many years to comfort a troubled child, or to meet his physical need—changed your plans frequently to meet an emergency, to help husband or a child—and with few words of encouragement some days.

Yes, you clean, sew, bake, cook, scrub, wash, and iron clothes—act as children's referee—care for scratches and wounds—drive different family members to their activities—attend ball games, PTA, husband's boss's picnic, and so on and on! At night you just stop. Your job never ends. You repeat the process the next day—and the next —*and the next.*

You receive no salary—yet are worth at least ninety dollars per hour as chef, nursemaid, psychiatrist, laundress,

147

cleaning woman, interior decorator, and chauffeur—all rolled into one!

Is it worth it? Why bother?

## A Choice

Many women are asking these questions.

For some, the answer is to avoid marriage and motherhood.

Others choose wifehood and motherhood with reservations. They continue pretty much their own life. Homemaking for them is merely a sideline.

Some choose homemaking, but gripe all day long. "I'm stuck between these four walls . . . I'm wasting my talents . . . If only . . . ."

Others try various escapisms: excessive phone calls, hours of TV watching, radio serials, outside activities, alcoholism, drugs.

Some enter into marriage purely on a businesslike basis: "I'll only do my share. I'll demand equal rights. No husband or children will monopolize my time and talents."

## Covenant of Love

Other homemakers accept marriage and parenthood as a covenant of love—not merely a legal contract.

Love cheerfully does "with her might what her hands find to do."

"Work is love made visible," speaks the poet Gibran.

Love enjoys what you are doing, as you do it.

A resolve to accept this attitude transformed Betsy's life, and her entire household. She hated housework—was always thinking ahead—quickly doing the dishes so she could run through the cleaning and get the work out of the way.

Then curl up in a corner with a book—grumbling when anyone interrupted her. This was her former pattern.

Now Betsy realizes that her hatred rubbed off on the family, making them unhappy. She has learned to enjoy each task as she does it. She enjoys smoothing the pillows and pulling the sheets straight.

"It's worth every moment I put into it," smiles Betsy. "My life is now filled with a tranquility I had never thought possible with four small children. Keeping house no longer is a trap. I now create an atmosphere of contentment and order, while enjoying the simple daily duties, and finding pleasure in the things as I see and do them. My husband is much happier, and wants to come home to us since I've learned to enjoy housekeeping."

## PROPER PERSPECTIVE

Betsy is aware that housekeeping is not an end in itself. It is only a means to an end. Family and home cannot exist without housekeeping. Housekeeping is only a part of being a homemaker but an essential part.

"The homemaker's program is to promote harmony and happy family relations and, in each member of her family, a sense of well-being. A homemaker's efficiency in doing housework is only a small part of her measurement as a wife and a mother," say Henry R. Brandt and Homer E. Dowdy in *Building a Christian Home*.

Orderliness and organization are important—but in its proper perspective.

Unfortunately, the modern American girl is a stranger to it. Untrained and lacking the skills, she's swamped after marriage. She's fearful and unsure of herself. She makes mistakes. She hates to reveal her inadequacies. She's often unaware of its importance, so abandons it for "greener pastures."

## Helps Make a House a Home

Cleaning floors, washing windows, cooking, doing the laundry, and other chores are necessary tasks needed to make a house a home—to make it livable and comfortable —to make it a place just for you and your family—a place shut out from the hurts of today's world—a place where there's warmth, love, and acceptance—a place of protection.

"Home is the laboratory of life"—where persons grow—where a helpless newborn infant develops—where the growing child and adults interact and learn to be persons—learn to care, to confront, to comfort, to love, to share, to be responsible persons, serving God and man.

Very important, in this process of making "a house a home," is the homemaker's attitudes while she does the daily tasks. A recent survey indicates that the mother's attitudes and approach to her role set the stage for the mood of the family. The focus then is not on unpleasant tasks but on the goals. This is true in any career. The nurse focuses on her goals of meeting the patients' needs and being a part of the healing—not on bedpans and changing sheets. The secretary focuses on doing a good job for her boss, not on erasures, correcting mistakes, running errands, and clearing up her desk.

## Freedom

The mature woman finds freedom within limits—within the limits of her choice. "Persons who elect to play the maternal role must accept some restrictions on their activities. To combine child care successfully with a second career requires either a stable mother-substitute in the home or a job that can be pursued in the home or on a part-time basis. Biology does place role restrictions on women. But it is not the biology of women themselves; it is the biologically based emotional needs of children that are demanding and undeniable,'' declares Jane Beckman Lancaster in *Quote*.

Becky senses her children's needs: "It is so tempting to go out and get a job when all your neighbors are doing it. But then, I think of my three children, ages eleven, nine, and six. I see so many unhappy, confused children today because their parents are too busy with their own lives and interests. They don't consider their children's wants and feelings important because they are children. I try to treat my children's feelings with respect and concern.''

## CHILDREN ENJOY HOME

To help raise a mature son and daughter who enjoy life, who are worthy citizens, who are able to establish good homes, who love and serve Jesus Christ makes many demands on a mother. It requires much sincere effort, tender concern, and self-giving, and self-discipline.

You may be involved in a part-time career, in voluntary service, in church and community activities. Good, but give priority to your choice of homemaker—man's helpmate and mother to your children. After you have met these responsibilities (and they do change with varying ages and stages of the family), you can give more of yourself to other areas. When mother is there to share, to listen and to care, children enjoy coming home, enjoy bringing their friends. They find security in her warmth and presence.

". . . the strongest kind of family [is] when people are

constantly around to help strengthen each other's inse-curities and defenses against loneliness," writes Robert Remmer, the novelist, in *Quote*.

When she relinquishes her homemaking duties, the family is unhappy.

Troublesome Johnny remarked to his teacher, "I don't want to go home. Everything's a mess. I can't find my clothes or my books."

In some communities, along with remedial reading classes, authorities have set up a Homemaker Program where a mature woman relates to the mother of a predelin-quent child in the home. She gains the mother's confidence and helps her do the simple housekeeping chores. She teaches her how to clean floors, prepare nourishing meals, make the home attractive, how to care for clothes, and how to relate in meaningful ways to the children.

Within a six weeks' period, the children no longer were problem children at school. Secure at home, they were se-cure at school.

## THE TEACHER

Former FBI director J. Edgar Hoover once commented on the home:

"There is no synthetic replacement for a decent home life. Our high crime rate, particularly among juveniles, is directly traceable to a breakdown in moral fiber—to the disintegration of home and family life. Religion and home life are supplementary. Each strengthens the other. It is seldom that a solid and wholesome home life can be found in the absence of religious inspiration."

There can be no more noble career than building good lives. True values are caught early in life as children and parents interact in work, play, worship, service, as they communicate with each other.

Children learn from parents' exemplary living, from guidance, from discipline, and from responsibility.

Through family relationships a child learns concepts of God—His forgiveness, love, mercy, care, and protection. When parents live out their faith and love to God, when He is real in their lives and homes, children learn who He is.

When children become faithful followers of Jesus Christ and worthy citizens, it's worth all the sacrifices and work.

## DIFFICULT

"To be a mother is difficult and dangerous, but no one can replace her," says psychoanalyst Florida Scott Maxwell in *Women and Sometimes Men*. She's disturbed because women fail to see how important they are. They're almost unlimited in their power to do good, *and to do harm*. Mostly done at home, in private, only they themselves control this power.

To give direction to family, to initiate projects, to discipline, to teach, to direct activities requires wisdom and skills and commitment. It's a worthy goal.

Anthropologist Margaret Mead says that through the ages, woman has always been there to give continuity to life. Woman heals the wounds, encourages, shares, and motivates.

It's not easy, but possible as Mary comments:

"When I'm low—tired of cleaning and washing and organizing preschoolers and fatigue almost overrules my patience, the old devil gets in there and presents me as a failure . . . a no-good mom and wife. He often tempts me to drop it all and get away in a full-time job.

"But then I stop, pray, and get him with some gems I've heard from 'Heart to Heart' program and some verses. You see, my husband is not a Christian. But he's getting closer; and I know through my daily life, and prayers (yours helping) and with PTL (patient, tender love), he will soon be won!"

"It's worth it all—to have a happy Christian family."

## Minor Tasks Important

Women's world today seems dominated by major achievements in academics, in technology, in science. But our communities would be hopeless—and helpless—without homemakers who spend many hours playing the minor parts—washing dishes, sweeping floors, washing and mending clothes, rocking babies, buying groceries, and performing dozens of other commonplace tasks.

These activities are not their goals, not ends in themselves, but means to an end—a comfortable home, a happy responsive family.

Many a person has performed his tasks well, has achieved fame because a mother, a wife, brilliantly played her behind-the-scene role.

Abraham Lincoln once remarked, "All that I am or hope to be, I owe to my angel mother."

"Her children rise up, and call her blessed; her husband also, and he praiseth her" (*see* Proverbs 31:28).

The key to your contentment and joy is your attitude toward yourself—your role—others—and God.

## The Spirit's Call

"I want to serve the Lord. Here I am stuck with my family!" someone protests.

Many years ago, when our three boys were small (they

came to us within four years), I believed "activity" was a proof of commitment to God and of a Spirit-filled life. I wanted to do things "for the Lord." Instead, I found myself busy meeting the children's and my husband's needs. I determined to be a "Mary" and sit at Jesus' feet—read his Word—learning and listening to Him, in order to "hear" what He wanted me to do!

You can imagine my frustrations with cooking meals, bathing babies, washing and ironing, soothing hurts —inwardly protesting the daily duties so necessary to family living.

One day the Lord spoke loud and clear through an elderly sister with these words, "Don't measure your depth of spirituality by activity or full-time service. When duty calls, that's the voice of the Spirit."

That proved to be my guide—my balance—my source of contentment and peace when tempted to chuck housekeeping responsibilities, with "Why bother?"

Those pressured days with young children are past. But in today's life as homemaker, pastor's wife, and radio speaker, I still use the guideline given to me by the dear sister.

Laurie confesses:

"I think in my case and in that of many housewives today, especially in suburban communities, the problem is not so much boredom as frustration. I feel frustrated because I never seem to finish my housework —the house is never all straightened up and spic-and-span at one time. It's an eight room, two and one-half bathroom house and I do all the work with only sporadic help from the children. Added to this is the constant taxi service which suburban housewives are afflicted with. Schools, churches, music lessons, doctors' and dentists' offices are not close by and we have no city buses. Therefore, all this taxiing has to be done by the housewife. There is school busing, but I'm speaking of extracurricular activities.

"I often think of the phrase 'order out of chaos' and often wish I could bring order out of the chaos of my housework. The problem here seems to be a superfluity of possessions such as toys, furniture, books, and magazines—all of which have to be put in places that often don't exist.

"I'm always telling myself and anyone else who will listen that I hate housework. Actually that's not true. What I really hate is organization which I'm poor at because that involves making decisions which is also not my forte. I think what I'd really like to be is a paid housekeeper with somebody else organizing my jobs!

"The idea of doing my work 'for the Lord' used to puzzle me very much. I could see a minister or a missionary or a doctor in Christian service doing this, but couldn't see how washing dishes, making beds, and mopping floors could be of any glorification of the Lord. But now I'm beginning to see that it is a part of stewardship—that we are supposed to care for that with which we are entrusted. I'm afraid I am often a very poor steward.

"I think another cause of frustration among educated housewives is their feeling that their education has been wasted if all they do is menial tasks that it doesn't take an education to perform.

"In spite of all these negative aspects I've expressed, I can think of no greater satisfaction than to be a housewife. There is nothing that can give you more pride than a good, Christian husband and fine, intelligent, interesting children who also think seriously of their Christian obligations. Also there's no greater happiness than the creativity of setting a beautiful table, decorating a birthday cake, preparing a good meal, decorating a room attractively and making the windows and furniture shine!

"By golly, I've written myself out of that frustration!"

## A UNIQUE RESPONSIBILITY

It is true—a woman can handle most of men's jobs, and do it well. But homemaking is uniquely hers. She can quit her other job and the work goes on. Not so with homemaking.

In her challenging book *Sixpence in Her Shoe,* author Phyllis McGinley so aptly stated ". . . it is as mothers and wives and householders that we make our unique contribution to humanity . . . the home is the world's end and its beginning—and that only women can properly create it."

The women of the greatest power and strength in today's world are not the names flashed on today's screens or in the news media, but rather the women in your community and mine who give themselves to their womanliness and to the responsibilities of mothers and helpmeets of their husband.

They help mold the character of our nation as they guide and train individual persons to Jesus Christ—the Truth, the Way of Rightness, and the Life. A writer in *The Union Signal* says, "If the time should ever come when women are not Christians and their houses not homes, then we shall have lost the chief cornerstones on which civilization rests."

## TRUE JOY

It's a paradox but true. The one who gives self, time, energy, and talents to help others finds happiness. The wife who is a helper to her husband and adapts to his ways because she loves him and her Lord, finds fulfillment and joy. The mother who gives herself to meet the children's needs receives her rewards. To paraphrase Francis of Assisi:

> In giving, she receives,
> In loving, she's loved.
> In understanding, she's understood.
> In showing appreciation, she's appreciated.
> In meeting another's needs, her needs are met.
> In accepting, she's accepted.
> In making others happy, she finds happiness.

With Jesus Christ as the center in your life, you can do even the most routine task "as unto Him." You no longer are a self-pleaser. You now are a Jesus-pleaser. With Him you can experience the joy of housekeeping.

---

Dear Reader:

I've enjoyed coming to you through the pages of this little book. Perhaps some of Marge and Jane and Pam's frustrations are yours also. If your situation is similar, but yet the answer doesn't seem to quite fit you, just write it all down—how it looks to you—how you feel—your reactions and attitudes, and send it to Heart to Heart, Harrisonburg, Virginia 22801.

There is no "pat" answer for every situation. Each homemaker has her own unique problem because each personality is complex and intricately different. However unique your problem is, together, through prayer and God's Word, we can find answers.

Peace and Joy,

*Ella May Miller*

# Index